First edition for North America and the Philippines published in 2013 by
Barron's Educational Series, Inc.

© RotoVision SA, Sheridan House,
114 Western Road, Hove,
East Sussex BN3 1DD, England

All inquiries should be addressed to:
Barron's Educational Series, Inc.
250 Wireless Boulevard
Hauppauge, New York 11788
www.barronseduc.com

ISBN: 978-1-4380-0102-9

Library of Congress Control No. 2011946188

Image credits for Contents, clockwise from top left:
Blanket coat. *House of Fraser*
Dress. *Family Affairs.* Cardigan. *Licia Florio*
Numph top. *MyLabel*
Turban. *Siel Davos*

Printed in China

9 8 7 6 5 4 3 2 1

Vintage Pattern Selector

THE SEWER'S GUIDE TO CHOOSING AND USING RETRO STYLES

Jo Barnfield

Contents

Patterns and keys

Printable patterns and sewing instructions for 15 garments are included on the CD that accompanies this book. In the book you will find diagrams of the finished garment, key measurements for the various pattern sizes, a sample pattern, and illustrated step-by-step sewing instructions.

KEY TO SEWING INSTRUCTIONS

In the illustrations that accompany the sewing instructions, the right side of the fabric is indicated without a texture, and the wrong side with a texture, as shown below. The numbers in the text link to the numbers identifying the illustrations.

Right side

Wrong side

KEY TO GARMENT PATTERNS

Refer to individual size tables, given alongside the sample patterns in the book, for actual measurements.

Extra large (XL)

—— XL cut line

--- XL stitch line

Large (L)

—— L cut line

--- L stitch line

Medium (M)

—— M cut line

--- M stitch line

Small (S)

—— S cut line

--- S stitch line

One size fits all

—— Cut line

--- Stitch line

Finding and printing your pattern

This symbol identifies the 15 patterns provided on the disc that accompanies this book. The number of the page on which the sample pattern appears in the book corresponds to the number used to identify it on the disc. For example, to find the pleated skirt pattern that appears on page 67, look on the disc for the pattern labeled 67. Pattern labels appear on the sample patterns in the book, but not on the printable patterns on the disc. Refer to the sample pattern in the book if you need guidance as to pattern pieces, stitch lines, grainlines, and fold lines.

Do not scale the patterns when printing. Each pattern has been tiled for printing onto Letter / A4 paper; each tile measures 180 (w) x 250mm (h) [c. 7$\frac{3}{32}$ (w) x 9$\frac{27}{32}$in (h)]. When you press "print," the number of pages required to fit the whole pattern will automatically print.

Before assembling your pattern, cut each page to the correct size, following the cut lines. These are indicated with scissor icons.

To assemble your pattern follow the letter and number in the top left-hand corner of each page, starting top left and following row by row from left to right, as shown in the sample opposite.

A1	A2	A3	A4	A5	A6
B1	B2	B3	B4	B5	B6
C1	C2	C3	C4	C5	C6
D1	D2	D3	D4	D5	D6
E1	E2	E3	E4	E5	E6

Timeline: *1920s to 1970s*

1920s

INNOVATIONS AND TRENDS
Flesh-colored stockings.

SILHOUETTES
The slender, flat-chested, drop-waisted look became the desired silhouette of the bright young things of the 1920s. The cloche hat, with its helmetlike fit, complemented the close-cropped hairstyles of the period.

BARE SKIN
Arms were bared not only for the evening, but also for the day; legs covered in beige stockings were visible up to the knee.

HEMLINES
Dresses and skirts featured dipping and handkerchief hemlines in lightweight, floaty fabrics.

1930s

INNOVATIONS AND TRENDS
The zipper, cowl necks, bias cutting, halterneck styles, and leisurewear.

SILHOUETTES
In the 1930s there was a return to a more genteel, ladylike appearance. Rounded busts and waistline curves were back in fashion. The cloche hat remained popular alongside perkily angled brimmed hats with matching gloves.

BARE SKIN
There was a passion for sunbathing and leisurewear. Women worked on their tans and showed them off under full-length backless evening dresses.

HEMLINES
Skirts were frequently longer at the back than the front. Below-the-knee pleats and godets fell from panels to give fullness at the hemline.

1940s

INNOVATIONS AND TRENDS
Padded shoulders and pants for women.

SILHOUETTES
During the war years, fashion became utilitarian, and women adopted a make-do-and-mend attitude to their clothing. Long hair was pinned up and worn in snoods and headscarfs or topped with a statement hat made from nonrationed materials and trims.

BARE SKIN
Nylon stockings were in such short supply that many women went bare-legged, sometimes resorting to painting seams down their legs to mimic sheer hose.

HEMLINES
Dresses reached knee length, even for eveningwear. This suited the vogue for swing dancing and complied with the fabric rationing of the era.

1950s

INNOVATIONS AND TRENDS
Sack and tent-line dresses and coats.

SILHOUETTES
In 1947, Dior introduced "the New Look," which featured the longer lengths and fuller skirts that grew in popularity during the 1950s. The sleek chic look worn by the likes of Audrey Hepburn was also widely adopted. Turbans returned to vogue as did pancake hats, which sat flat on top of the head and mimicked turn-of-the-century styles.

BARE SKIN
Stockings were back in circulation, but short sleeves and sleeveless tops became iconic of a more glamorous look. Necklines became more revealing, with cowl necks and fewer collars and ruffles at the neck.

HEMLINES
Skirts and dresses were knee-length or lower, with the fuller skirt remaining popular.

1960s

INNOVATIONS AND TRENDS
The mini-skirt, pantyhose, pillbox hats, and bold printed fabrics.

SILHOUETTES
Building on the sleek look of the late 1950s, the 1960s saw a growing popularity in short, close-fitting A-line dresses and tight, narrow pants. Pillbox hats perched on the back of the head and matching gloves were popular, reflecting Jackie Kennedy's preppy style.

BARE SKIN
Dresses were often worn with brightly colored pantyhose, more usually teamed with knee-high boots. Sleeveless styles were popular.

HEMLINES
This was the decade of the mini-skirt, with hemlines creeping well above the knee.

1970s

INNOVATIONS AND TRENDS
Ethnic-inspired fashion, platform shoes, and hotpants.

SILHOUETTES
Halterneck catsuits and straight or flared Empire-line maxi dresses with statement sleeves were popular. Hats, when worn, were often wide-brimmed. Hat wearing generally declined during the 1970s and hair was often worn long, straight, and uncoiffured.

BARE SKIN
Halter and pinafore necklines and ultra-short hemlines teamed with platform boots or shoes contrasted with long maxi dresses.

HEMLINES
Hemlines varied widely throughout this era, from floor-length maxi dresses and wide-legged pants though to mini- and micro-skirted styles.

CHAPTER 1

Dresses

Dress styles and lengths evolved rapidly during the twentieth century. The so-called flappers of the 1920s wore knee-length, dropped-waist dresses that, although daringly short, also required a flat-chested, boyish silhouette. The 1930s introduced a slinky Hollywood-inspired glamor, and floor-length bias-cut gowns were the signature style of the decade. The 1940s, dominated by war and austerity, saw functional wear and military-inspired looks. The 1950s saw a return to femininity, and the distinctive dress shape of that era featured a narrow waist contrasted with a full skirt. Women of the 1960s embraced the short, sleeveless shift dress as a style both elegant and versatile, while the 1970s saw both hippie-style maxi dresses and the disco chic of the bias-cut wrap dress. Dresses have since been a stalwart in many women's wardrobes, with easy-going styles for day and glamorous numbers for night.

Shirt dress.
(Model's own)

The flapper dress: 1920s

The flapper dress became the garment of choice for liberal, free-thinking women in the era after World War I. Largely influenced by French fashion, particularly Coco Chanel, flapper dresses were youthful and boyish. The style was straight and loose-fitting, sleeveless, with the waistline dropping to the hips. Skirt lengths started at the ankles but gradually became shorter; by around 1926, hemlines were high enough to reveal the knees. By the end of the 1920s, hemlines had dropped once again.

Flapper dresses were made from durable fabrics, often in basic colors, and had varied necklines. A day dress might have a V-neck or scoop neck, while a party dress often had two layers: an opaque underdress with a scoop neck, and an overlay with a boatneck. Party dresses also featured trims and finishes on the overlay such as beading, fringing, lace, and rhinestones. Because the straight shift construction of the flapper dress was less complicated than many earlier fashions, women in the 1920s became more successful at home dressmaking.

WHO: A result of the flapper movement and influenced by Coco Chanel and French fashion.

WHY: Since flapper dresses had simpler designs than those before them, it was easier to produce up-to-date flapper fashions at home using dress patterns.

VARIATIONS: Day dresses featured V or scoop necks; party dresses often had two layers with scoop and boatnecks, as well as trims and finishes.

SIMILAR STYLES: Drop-waisted dress, page 22

PATTERNS TO MATCH WITH: 1920s slip, page 114

Navy sequin flapper dress. *Ruby Ray*

Black dress (www.Kambriel.com). *Kambriel Macaluso*

Style and uses, then and now

FABRIC

Then: Netting was often used as an overlay to support heavy beading, sequins, and rhinestones. Rayon and georgette, which hug the body, were used to give a boyish shape. Organza was used to give dresses a stiffer and puffier shape.

Now: Similar fabrics are used, although fashion items tend to be made from cheaper fabrics such as nylon, rayon, and polyester.

LENGTH

Then: Skirt lengths varied from ankle-length to knee-length.

Now: Flapper dresses tend to be worn shorter today, and are often around knee-length or slightly higher.

STYLE

Then: Flapper dresses in the 1920s had a loose-fitting style making them suitable for a variety of body shapes. They often featured a variety of trims and finishes.

Now: Flapper dresses today tend to pay homage to original 1920s styles, although they are generally more simple and practical in style.

COLORS

Then: Flapper dresses tended to be neutral, black, or in a bold, vibrant color such as red.

Now: Modern flapper dresses tend to pay homage to the 1920s style, and similar colors are used.

MATCHED WITH

Then: Flapper dresses were most often worn with strands of pearls, feathered headbands, cloche hats, T-bar shoes, stockings, and shoulder-length satin gloves. Hair was short and cut into a bob and heavy makeup was worn (particularly dark eyes, dark lips, and some contouring).

Now: Similar accessories should be worn to achieve the vintage flapper style, but for a more modern look, pair your flapper dress with heels, pendant necklaces, a blazer or leather jacket, and metallic bangles.

NOW

V-neck sequined flapper dress. *P.A.R.O.S.H.*

NOW

Beaded flapper dress. *House of Fraser*

SEWING TIPS

- Keep the design simple and uncomplicated.

- For a fringed dress, use the same color for fringe and dress, or mix things up with a metallic fringe over black or a black fringe over a bold color.

The little black dress: 1920s on

4429

Miss
Size 18
Bust 38

50¢ IN CANADA 60¢

Simplicity Printed Pattern

Jiffy dress 2 main pattern pieces

easy-cut easy-sew

THEN

Reacting to the brash colors worn by ladies at the opera, Coco Chanel "imposed black" with the design of a narrow little black dress (LBD) in the 1920s, marking the birth of one of fashion's perpetual favorites.

When a sketch of Chanel's LBD appeared in *American Vogue* in 1926 it was predicted to become "a uniform, as widely recognized as a Ford automobile: fast and sleek and discreet." Conforming with Chanel's desire to design functional clothing, the style suited all shapes, and was appropriate for both day and eveningwear, which has much to do with its lasting appeal.

After World War II, the LBD enjoyed a design overhaul when Christian Dior changed the shape of fashion with what *Harper's Bazaar* coined "the New Look," a style defined by full skirts, nipped-in waists, pronounced busts, and, crucially, a wealth of material. In the 1960s, the LBD was slimmed down thanks to the arrival of Mary Quant's mini-skirt. The style remains popular today—a trusted fashion staple for women of all tastes.

WHO: Coco Chanel is widely credited with transforming the little black dress from mourning attire to a fashion staple. A sketch of her dropped-waist narrow black dress, worn with pearls, appeared in *American Vogue* in 1926.

WHY: A chic and simple style that never goes out of fashion, the LBD has remained a classic choice for formal events, having been designed to flatter all shapes.

VARIATIONS: Black dresses were as varied as the women who wore them, made from luxurious or simple fabrics. They're now a central wardrobe choice for just about any occasion.

SIMILAR STYLES: Flapper dress, page 12; Peter Pan collar, page 46; pencil skirt, page 60

PATTERNS TO MATCH WITH: Mini dress, page 30

NOW

Black lace dress. *Ruby Ray*

NOW

Black dress with peplum. *FCUK*

Style and uses, then and now

FABRIC

Then: Elegant materials such as cotton, lace, tulle, and silks were traditionally used to create this design classic. The advent of synthetic materials made the style more widely available and affordable in the 1940s and 1950s. Sheer fabrics and velvet became prevalent in the 1960s.

Now: Slinky, sheer, and sparkle-detail fabrics remain popular for eveningwear, while cotton and jersey styles prove more suitable for daytime looks.

LENGTH

Then: The narrow knee-length dress made popular by Chanel in the 1920s was lengthened and widened by Christian Dior's "New Look" in the late 1940s before shrinking with the advent of the mini-skirt in the 1960s.

Now: Most contemporary designs fall on or above the knee.

STYLE

Then: Long-sleeved, over-the-knee dresses were a top choice with socialites and performers in the 1920s and 1930s. Short sleeves, nipped-in waists, and full calf-length skirts helped celebrate a sense of fashion-forward fun and freedom in postwar Europe. In the 1960s, the style was assimilated into the mod look, with short black shift dresses becoming a staple for fashionable young women.

Now: Drawing on the most popular styles of the past century, the LBD now comes in all shapes and sizes, with vintage pieces very much in demand.

COLORS

Then: Chanel was reportedly repelled by the loud colors worn by ladies at the opera in the 1920s, "imposing black" to "wipe out everything else around." The color was also practical and was believed to suit all shapes.

Now: The appeal of the LBD remains strong today primarily because black is believed to flatter and slim the figure and to suit everyone.

MATCHED WITH

Then: Traditionally worn with pearls, the LBD was accessorized with simple yet glamorous jewelry throughout the early and midcentury period, and has boasted details such as bows, belts, and Peter Pan collars as the style evolved.

Now: With current designers still adhering to the "less-is-more" principle when it comes to the LBD, today's simple silhouettes are updated with design details such as bandeau, halterneck, and Peter Pan collar necklines and peplum waists.

SEWING TIPS

- When using a mix of black fabrics it is essential that you color-match your fabrics in natural daylight as black dyes come in a range of hues and tones.

- Don't overpress your garment as it is easy to create shine. Use a pressing cloth to protect the fabric.

- Invest in a lint roller. You will find it handy during the making of any black items.

NOW

Black dress with ruffle trims. *Vivetta*

Bias cutting: 1930s

1317 1933 Size **THEN**

Fashion designers of the 1930s moved away from the linear, gamine look of the 1920s in favor of softer silhouettes that accentuated feminine contours.

Bias-cut dresses are cut on the diagonal grain of the fabric, which causes the material to fall into a smooth, vertical drape; the designer can then easily manipulate the fabric into clinging folds. Bias-cut styles were often worn during the 1930s, frequently appearing on glamorous actresses in the Hollywood movies of that era. Bias-cut dresses had sleek, easy grace and smooth comfort, and followed the lines of the body, contributing to the trend toward natural lines. When the Duchess of Windsor (Wallis Simpson) married the former King Edward VIII in 1937, she wore a bias-cut dress and tailored jacket in silk crepe by American designer Mainbocher. As the duchess was a style icon of her time, this further cemented the trend's importance in fashion history.

Today, the bias-cut dress is still often worn for evening events, with figure-flattering designs often made in satin and silk. Longer-length styles remain sought after, and the patterns and fabrics used to make such dresses have not changed much from those of the 1930s.

WHO: Madeleine Vionnet perfected the bias-cut look; Mainbocher came to attention for designing the Duchess of Windsor's wedding dress in 1937.

WHY: The bias-cut dress evoked femininity after the understated austerity and boyish looks of the 1920s. The style was also perfectly paired with the new backless gowns that appeared during the decade.

VARIATIONS: Shorter crepe-de-chine styles are often seen in summer, while handkerchief designs became popular in the 1970s.

SIMILAR STYLES: N/A

PATTERNS TO MATCH WITH: Circle skirt, page 70

NOW

Tweed dress. *Ruby Ray*

NOW

Asymmetrical chiffon dress. *Ruby Ray*

Style and uses, then and now

FABRIC

Then: Body-clinging fabrics such as satin, charmeuse, and crepe de chine made from silk or "artificial silk" viscose were used to make formal evening dresses.

Now: Lightweight fabrics such as viscose and polyester are used for bias-cut styles today, sometimes with elastane. Satin and silks are still used for eveningwear, and printed fabric is also often used.

LENGTH

Then: Dresses typically sat below the ankle and fell close to the ground.

Now: Lengths vary depending on the occasion. Dresses now often sit above the knee.

STYLE

Then: A design for the wealthy, the bias-cut dress was worn for formal affairs and often signaled high social status. The working class also attempted to adapt the style.

Now: Designs often feature decorative detail such as gems and sequins for eveningwear. Dresses also come in a variety of designs, including tea dresses and pencil skirt silhouettes.

COLORS

Then: Dresses were often made in soft pink, ivory, and peach tones. With satin, the sheen added an extra delicacy.

Now: With an extensive range of lightweight fabrics now available, the choice is much broader. Dresses can be dip-dyed, black, or printed. Delicate satins are still popular, with ivory bias panels often used on wedding dresses.

MATCHED WITH

Then: Worn with fur stoles, elegant shoes, and chic sparkling jewelry, bias-cut dresses were very much designed for evening attire.

Now: Worn for a variety of events, the bias-cut dress can be teamed with boots and cardigans for a casual day look or stiletto heels for evening glamor.

SEWING TIPS

- Cutting garments on the diagonal requires more fabric than straight-grain work. Remember to allow for this when purchasing fabric.

- Lay your pattern pieces at 45 degrees to the selvage and take great care not to stretch the fabric during construction.

- Sandwich your fabric between sheets of dressmaking paper and cut through paper and fabric in one.

- Bias cutting can be used to great effect with a patterned fabric.

NOW

Bias-cut maxi dress with self-tie waist. *A/Wear*

The halterneck: 1930s / 1950s / 1970s

THEN

The halterneck consists of a single piece of fabric, or two pieces tied together, that runs behind the neck. Originally popularized by designer Madeleine Vionnet in the 1930s, the halterneck was used with her bias-cutting technique to create slinky and revealing backless evening dresses. The halterneck returned to popularity in the 1950s, when a square-necked style with a fitted and structured bodice was popular for both day and eveningwear on cotton sundresses and more elaborate evening gowns. It returned again in the 1970s with a slinky, relaxed, draping style that flattered a lean silhouette.

The halterneck top is still a popular style for day and evening, but can be much less structured than a 1950s version. Made from a soft jersey fabric, it can have the drape of a cowl, and be worn with jeans or shorts during the summer. Modern halterneck evening gowns made from satin might still echo the classic lines of Vionnet's original design.

WHO: Madeleine Vionnet is credited with creating the first halterneck styles.

WHY: Backless tops are elegant but revealing.

VARIATIONS: Cutaway arms, bandeau halter.

SIMILAR STYLES: 1940s slip, page 120

PATTERNS TO MATCH WITH: Wide-legged pants, page 82

NOW

Knitted halterneck. *Missoni*

Style and uses, then and now

FABRIC

Then: Vionnet's original halternecks were made in silk and satin, cut on the bias to create a body-skimming silhouette. In the 1950s, cotton was a common fabric for day dresses, with heavy brocades and satin for eveningwear. In the 1970s daytime dresses were cotton or jersey.

Now: Modern stretch jersey fabrics are much more forgiving and create a flattering drape for halterneck tops or evening dresses.

LENGTH

Then: 1970s halternecks were maxi dresses, coming down to the ankles.

Now: Today there is no particular length; this varies according to style and fashion.

STYLE

Then: Bias-cut evening dresses in the 1930s were strictly for the slim and rich. In the 1950s, halter tops were commonly a teenage fashion; older women were more likely to wear halternecks on evening dresses. 1970s evening dresses were figure-hugging and often slashed to the thigh.

Now: Halter tops have a sportier feel when made in modern fabrics. Modern strapless bras and supportwear mean they are no longer confined to teenagers. The neckline is often used on swimwear.

COLORS

Then: Vionnet was fond of pale shades such as ivory or duck-egg blue for her evening gowns. In the 1950s, brightly colored or printed cottons in checks and polka dots were popular, while florals were popular in the 1970s.

Now: Colors are limited only by imagination and what fabrics are available. Neutral shades such as gray, black, and white make the top versatile enough to be worn with a variety of other colors.

MATCHED WITH

Then: Diamonds and evening gloves were perfect partners for a 1930s evening gown. The 1950s reincarnation of the halter top was often teamed with Capri pants or circle skirts, and the 1970s maxi with large hats and sunglasses in the day and sparkling jewelry for eveningwear.

Now: Jeans make ideal casual daywear with a jersey halter top, while a halterneck could be dressed up for eveningwear with a pair of wide-legged palazzo pants. With such a revealing top, it is best to keep the bottom half fairly demure and team it with trousers or skirts of knee length or longer.

NOW

Tricolor body dress. *bonprix*

SEWING TIPS

- To convert a pattern into a halterneck style, baste the neckline pieces into place to make a fitting muslin and graft on extra fabric as the design dictates. Attach your strap with handstitches and adjust to the necessary length. Transfer this fabric pattern piece to paper for further cutting.

The natural waist: 1950s

NEW YORK PATTERN

PETTICOAT 1065 B

NEW YORK PATTERN Gold Seal Guaranteed Perfect

THEN

After the fabric restrictions and austere fashions necessitated by World War II, Christian Dior revolutionized the fashion world with the introduction of a new silhouette in which the waistline was raised to its natural position.

Dior's first spring collection, famously nicknamed "the New Look" by Carmel Snow, editor of *Harper's Bazaar*, featured silhouettes that were narrow and tailored, with pronounced shoulders, a nipped-in waist, and full skirts. The waist was natural in placement and this tight, often belted, look was prominent until the mid-1950s. Dior's name is one instantly associated with 1950s fashion.

The dirndl dress was another natural-waisted look that appealed to young women in the 1950s, and this most flattering of styles is still a popular choice on today's catwalks. Rather than the waistline sitting on top of a swathe of petticoats, the styles seen today are usually much softer, with the waist less exaggerated.

WHO: Christian Dior reintroduced the natural waistline after wartime austerity.

WHY: This is a flattering style that skims curves and creates a very feminine silhouette.

VARIATIONS: The full petticoat style, the straight pencil look, the poplin shirt dress, and the belted coat-dress.

SIMILAR STYLES: Circle skirt, page 62; pencil skirt, page 60

PATTERNS TO MATCH WITH: Prom dress, page 26; maxi dress, page 36

NOW

Natural waist highlighted with decorative band. *ASOS.com*

NOW

Chiffon dress. *Topshop*

Style and uses, then and now

FABRIC

Then: Wool was frequently used for day designs, with rayon, taffeta, and crepe popular choices for formal eveningwear.

Now: Stretch cotton for casual day dresses add a lightweight effect to the design, with elasticated detailing enhancing the nipped-in waist.

LENGTH

Then: Designs typically hung 13 to 15 inches (33 to 38cm) from the ground.

Now: Above-the-knee styles are more common, with knee-length designs also popular.

STYLE

Then: Fitted bodices prevailed and mid-calf-length, princess-line skirts were appealing. Older ladies enjoyed flecked wool tweed, while younger wearers embraced floral prints.

Now: Skinny belts subtly accentuate the small natural waistline, and fitted pencil-skirt dresses are often deemed the most becoming. Exaggerated shoulders are often used to complement this womanly silhouette.

COLORS

Then: Monochrome designs were most sought after and the "Little Black Dress" became a desirable choice. Color was prominent though, with pretty yellow and mauve fabrics becoming popular for the first time.

Now: Designers such as Erdem embrace this silhouette and keep the styling almost vintage with floral designs that incorporate a lot of green. The use of block color creates a very elegant interpretation of the look.

MATCHED WITH

Then: Often paired with fitted boned bodices, elbow-length satin gloves, stiffened petticoats, satin pointed shoes, and self-fabric buckled waist-belts, the look was refined and the silhouette elegant.

Now: The body-conscious look has been popular since the 1990s; the figure-hugging fabric being enhanced with a leather belt. High heels add to the curvaceous effect, with opaque tights a modern touch.

Natural waist highlighted with belt. *Marc Jacobs*

SEWING TIPS

- When sewing a fabric with natural stretch or working on bias-cut sections, add a narrow piece of tape as the waist seam is completed. This will ensure the waistline does not stretch or distort during wear.

- Add small strips of strain-grain fabric or chain stitch loops at the side seams to keep narrow belts in position.

Drop-waisted dress: 1920s

GARMENT SPEC

This drop-waisted dress has a relaxed fit and a pleated hip yoke. Suitable for fine, lightweight fabrics, such as lawn.

STYLE VARIATIONS

The scarf for this style can be worn loosely around the neck or used as a belt. Use a sheer fabric for this dress and add an opaque slip (pattern on page 114) to create a layered look reminiscent of the 1930s.

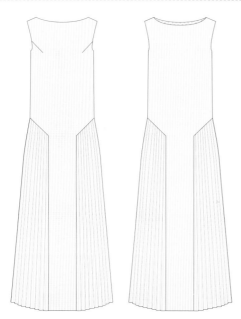

Front   Back

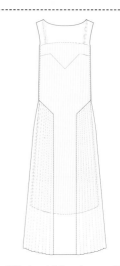

With sheer fabric and opaque slip

With belt

Sizes	S (in)	S (cm)	M (in)	M (cm)	L (in)	L (cm)	XL (in)	XL (cm)
Bust at armhole	36⁷⁄₁₆	92.6	38⁷⁄₁₆	97.6	40³⁄₈	102.6	42³⁄₈	107.6
Waist	36⁷⁄₁₆	92.6	38⁷⁄₁₆	97.6	40³⁄₈	102.6	42³⁄₈	107.6
Hem on seam	71⁵⁄₁₆	181.2	73⁵⁄₁₆	186.2	75¼	191.2	77¼	196.2
Shoulder	1⁷⁄₈	4.7	1¹⁵⁄₁₆	5	2¹⁄₁₆	5.3	2³⁄₁₆	5.6
CB length to hem	44⁹⁄₁₆	113.2	44¹³⁄₁₆	113.8	45¹⁄₁₆	114.4	45¼	115
Back neck on seam	12⁵⁄₈	31.9	12¹³⁄₁₆	32.5	13¹⁄₁₆	33.1	13¼	33.7
Front neck on seam	12¹⁄₁₆	30.7	12⁵⁄₁₆	31.3	12⁹⁄₁₆	31.9	12¹³⁄₁₆	32.5
CB to hipline	20⁵⁄₈	52.4	20⁷⁄₈	53	21⅛	53.6	21⅜	54.2
CB to knee line	35⁹⁄₁₆	90.4	35¹³⁄₁₆	91	36¹⁄₁₆	91.6	36⁵⁄₁₆	92.2

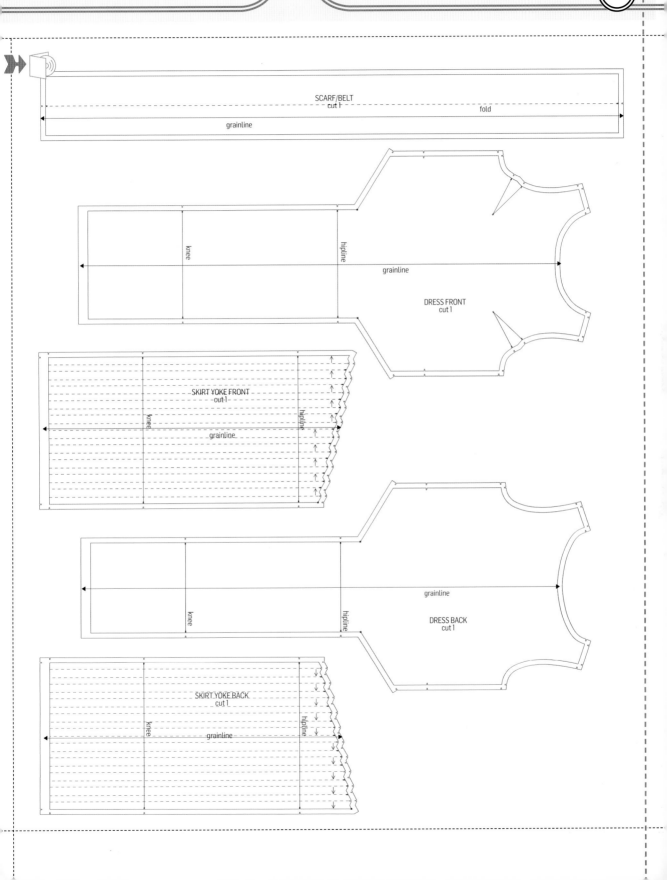

SCARF/BELT
— cut 1 —
fold
grainline

knee
hipline
grainline

DRESS FRONT
cut 1

SKIRT YOKE FRONT
— cut 1 —
knee
hipline
grainline

grainline

DRESS BACK
cut 1

knee
hipline

SKIRT YOKE BACK
cut 1
knee
hipline
grainline

PATTERN INSTRUCTIONS

(1) Sew the darts on the front panel and press the dart excess toward the side seam. (2) Pleat the skirt panels, ensuring that the pleat direction is followed; if pleated correctly, the pleats will form a box pleat at the side seam. (3) With right sides together, join the front skirt yoke to the front dress; pin to the first marking only and machine to this point. Lower the machine needle through the work and miter the dress section only; make sure that this snip stops short of the mark, or the corner will be destabilized. Keeping the machine needle through the work, pivot the yoke section and continue sewing to the hem. Press the seam closed, with seam allowances toward the side seam.

①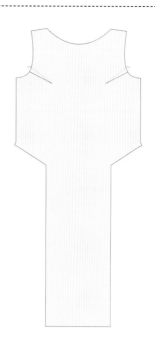

②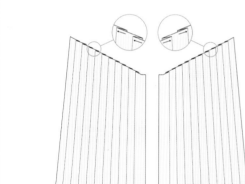

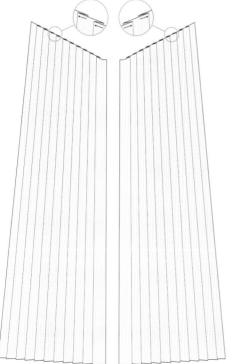

③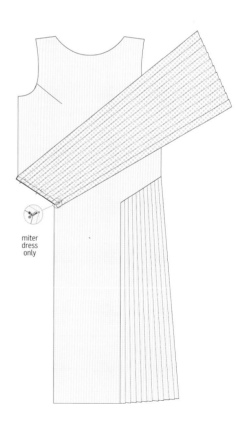

miter dress only

(4) Placing right sides together, sew the shoulder seam and press the seam allowances open. **(5)** With right sides together, sew the side seam. Take care when you reach the pleated yoke panel—fold the pleats out of the way of the seam line so they are not caught as you sew the side seam. Press the seam allowances open. **(6)** Finish the arm and neckline with a bound facing or a roll hem. **(7)** Fold the scarf in half and sew along the open edge, leaving a gap to facilitate turning out.

▶▶ PATTERN TIP

Transfer markings to the fabric with a tailor's tack or alternative marking technique, otherwise the angular hip yoke will be difficult to match and sew correctly.

④

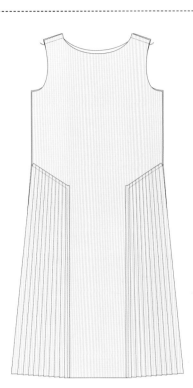

⑤

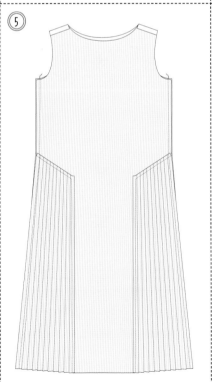

⑥

⑦

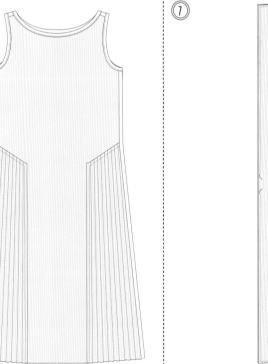

Prom dress: 1950s

▶ GARMENT SPEC

This dress has a fitted bodice and a box-pleated skirt. Suitable for medium-weight fabrics.

STYLE VARIATIONS

The collar can be cut in contrasting or matching fabric. Consider mounting the top collar with a layer of lace or discarding the collar and decorating the neckline with a bow or embroidery. You could also cut a circle skirt for this style (pattern on page 70). Measure the waist of the bodice and cut a circle skirt to match.

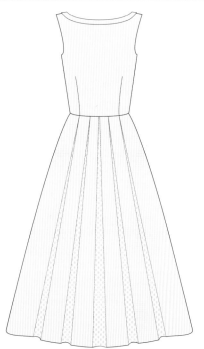

Front

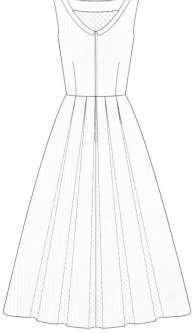

Back

Front

Back

Sizes	S (in)	S (cm)	M (in)	M (cm)	L (in)	L (cm)	XL (in)	XL (cm)
Bust at armhole	33¼	84.4	35³⁄₁₆	89.4	37³⁄₁₆	94.4	39⅛	99.4
Waist	26⅜	67	28⅜	72	30⁵⁄₁₆	77	32⁵⁄₁₆	82
Hem on seam	40⁹⁄₁₆	103	42½	108	44½	113	46⁷⁄₁₆	118
Shoulder	2¹⁄₁₆	5.2	2³⁄₁₆	5.5	2⁵⁄₁₆	5.8	2⅜	6.1
CB length to hem	24⅛	61.2	24⁵⁄₁₆	61.8	24⁹⁄₁₆	62.4	24¹³⁄₁₆	63
CB length to waistline	8¹⁄₁₆	20.4	8¼	21	8½	21.6	8¾	22.2
Back neck on seam	8⁹⁄₁₆	21.7	8¾	22.3	9	22.9	9¼	23.5
Front neck on seam	11¹⁵⁄₁₆	30.4	12³⁄₁₆	31	12⁷⁄₁₆	31.6	12¹¹⁄₁₆	32.2

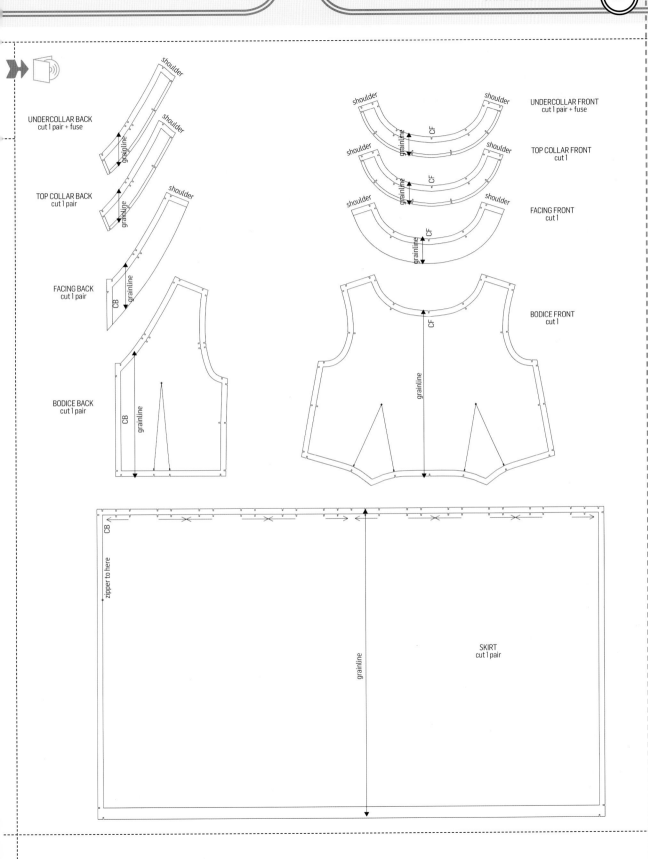

UNDERCOLLAR BACK
cut 1 pair + fuse

shoulder

shoulder

grainline

TOP COLLAR BACK
cut 1 pair

grainline

shoulder

FACING BACK
cut 1 pair

CB

grainline

BODICE BACK
cut 1 pair

CB

grainline

shoulder

shoulder

UNDERCOLLAR FRONT
cut 1 pair + fuse

CF

grainline

shoulder

shoulder

TOP COLLAR FRONT
cut 1

CF

grainline

shoulder

shoulder

FACING FRONT
cut 1

CF

grainline

CF

BODICE FRONT
cut 1

grainline

CB

zipper to here

SKIRT
cut 1 pair

grainline

PATTERN INSTRUCTIONS

(1) Prepare the collar. With right sides facing, sew the shoulder seams and press the seam allowances open. Repeat for the undercollar. **(2)** Using a ¼in (6mm) seam allowance, sew the top collar and undercollar with right sides together. Turn the collar to the right side, press, and set aside. **(3)** Prepare the facing: With RS together, sew the shoulder seams and press the seam allowances open. Neaten the lower edge with an overlock or a zigzag stitch. Set aside. **(4)** Sew the darts on the back bodice. **(5)** Sew the darts on the front bodice, then trim the darts (see page 160). **(6)** With right sides together, sew the shoulder and side seams. **(7)** Press the seam allowances open. Finish the armholes with a bound facing (see page 169).

PATTERN TIP

Do not over-press the pleats: steam gently and let the fullness fall through to the hem without constraining volume with rigid pleating.

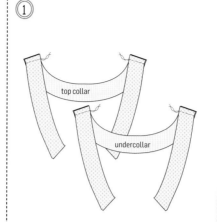

① top collar / undercollar

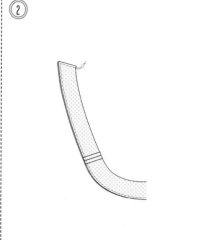

②

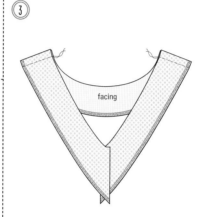

③ facing

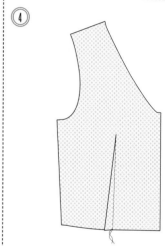

④

⑤

⑥

⑦ press SA open / bind arm

(8) Sew the center front seam on the skirt and press the seam allowances open. Pleat the skirt section, making sure you follow the pleat direction from the pattern piece. With RS together, sew the waist seam and press the seam allowances toward the neckline. Miter the corners on the bodice and skirt seam at CB to reduce bulk. Hem the skirt.

(9) Set the machine to its longest stitch and sew from CB neckline to zipper insertion point. Return the machine stitch to the usual stitch length, make a couple of backstitches to reinforce the opening, and sew to hem. Press the seam allowances open. Insert a concealed zipper (see page 176). Ensure the CB pleats are not caught as the zipper is stitched. You will need to stop stitching at the waist seam, raise the machine foot, and move the pleats clear of the work. Lower the needle and begin sewing below the waist seam. When the zipper is in position, unpick the basting stitches to release the opening.

(10) Turn work to the right side and lay the collar, with right sides uppermost, onto the bodice. Lay the facing, with right sides together, on top of the collar and bodice, sandwiching the collar between the bodice and the facing. Pin in place, matching notches.

(11) Sew through all layers around the front and back neckline edge, stopping at CB. Press the facing upward and understitch through the facing and seam allowances only. Grade the seam allowances to reduce bulk. Fold the facing into position, trim any excess, and hand-sew the facing edge to the zipper.

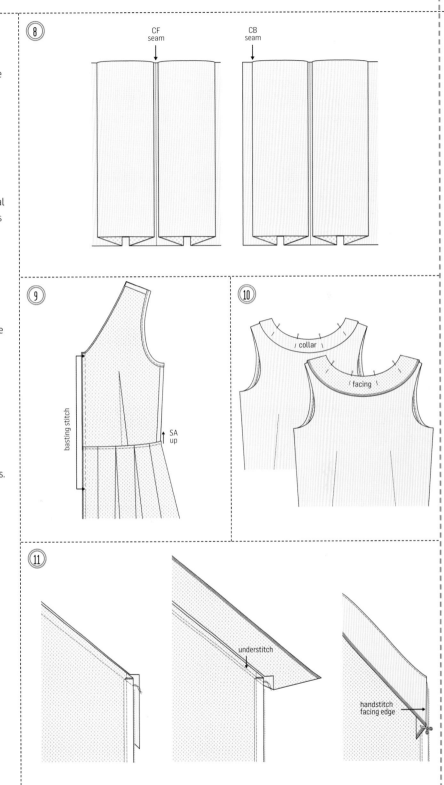

Mini dress: 1960s

GARMENT SPEC

This dress flares gently from the hip and has a tuck-detail yoke with a Peter Pan collar. Suitable for a variety of fabrics. Use bold print for the main body and plain fabric for the yoke panel for a bib-front look.

Sizes	S (in)	S (cm)	M (in)	M (cm)	L (in)	L (cm)	XL (in)	XL (cm)
Bust at armhole	35⁷⁄₁₆	90	37⅜	95	39⅜	100	41⁵⁄₁₆	105
Waist	27½	69.9	29½	74.9	31⁷⁄₁₆	79.9	33⁷⁄₁₆	84.9
Hem on seam	41³⁄₁₆	104.6	43⅛	109.6	45⅛	114.6	47¹⁄₁₆	119.6
Shoulder	3⅛	7.9	3¼	8.2	3⅜	8.5	3⁷⁄₁₆	8.8
CB length to hem	34	86.4	34¼	87	34½	87.6	34¾	88.2
Back neck on seam	9⅛	23.1	9⁵⁄₁₆	23.7	9⁹⁄₁₆	24.3	9¹³⁄₁₆	24.9
Front neck on seam	11⅝	29.5	11⅞	30.1	12¹⁄₁₆	30.7	12⁵⁄₁₆	31.3
Zipper length	21¼	54	21¼	54	21¼	54	21¼	54
Sleeve length ex cuff	23⁹⁄₁₆	59.9	23¾	60.3	23⅞	60.7	24¹⁄₁₆	61.1
Cuff width	1⅜	3.5	1⅜	3.5	1⅜	3.5	1⅜	3.5

Front   Back

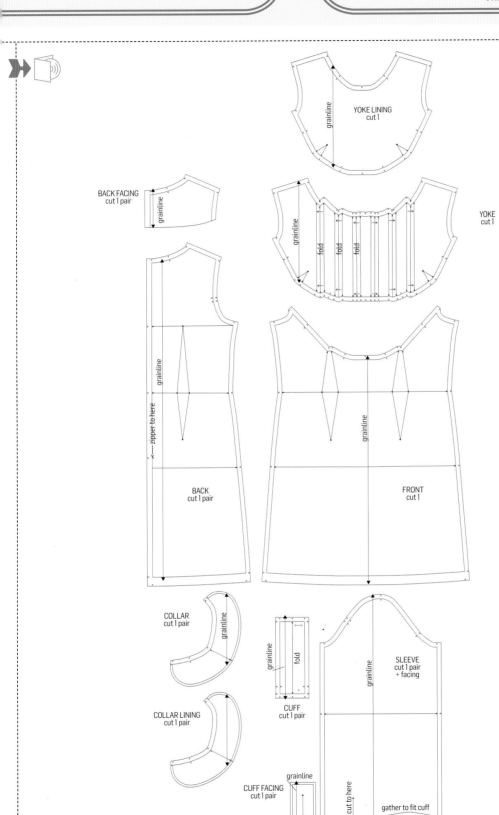

YOKE LINING
cut 1

grainline

BACK FACING
cut 1 pair

grainline

YOKE
cut 1

grainline

fold fold fold

grainline

zipper to here

BACK
cut 1 pair

grainline

FRONT
cut 1

COLLAR
cut 1 pair

grainline

grainline

fold

CUFF
cut 1 pair

grainline

SLEEVE
cut 1 pair
+ facing

COLLAR LINING
cut 1 pair

grainline

CUFF FACING
cut 1 pair

cut to here

gather to fit cuff

PATTERN INSTRUCTIONS

(1) First prepare the collar. With right sides together, sew the undercollar and top collar together with a ¼in (6mm) seam allowance. Due to the narrow seam allowance, you should not need to clip the curves unless the fabric is particularly bulky. Repeat for other side. **(2)** Prepare the facing. Sew darts on the yoke lining and, with right sides together, join the shoulder seams. Neaten the lower edge with an overlock or zigzag stitch. Press dart excess toward center front. Set aside. **(3)** Prepare the cuff. Set the machine to its longest stitch and sew a line of machine basting along one long edge. Return the stitch length to its usual setting. Fold the cuff in half lengthways with RS facing and stitch the short edge. Stitch along the short edge and along the open edge, stopping at the notch to create a turned-out underlap. Snip the seam allowance close, but not through the stitch line and turn the cuff to the right side. Press and add topstitching if desired. Set aside. **(4)** Prepare the sleeve facing. Miter the top edge and press a ¼in (6mm) seam allowance to the wrong side. Secure with a machine stitch. **(5)** Lay facing to sleeve with right sides together. Stitch from hem to drill hole approximately ⅛in (3mm) from the slit marking. Reduce the stitch length toward the top of the opening and make one or two machine stitches across the apex rather than pivoting the work, then sew back to the hem. Carefully cut through all layers along the slit opening, stopping close to the line of stitching. Turn the facing through to WS of sleeve and press into position. Edge-stitch the facing into place and blind stitch the upper edge into position if desired. Repeat for the other side.

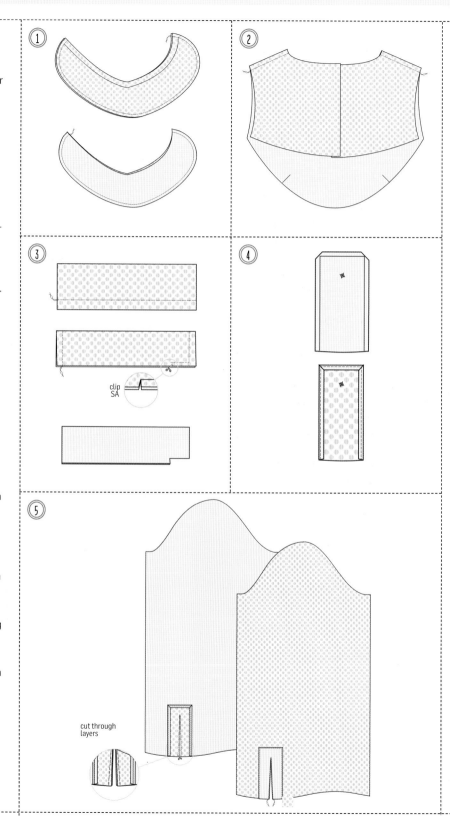

clip SA

cut through layers

(6) With right sides together, sew the sleeve underarm seam, then press the seam allowance open. Set the machine to the longest stitch and machine two lines of gathering stitch along the sleeve hem edge. Turn sleeve to WS and draw gathering stitch evenly to match the cuff measurement. Lay the open edge of the cuff without machine basting to the RS of the sleeve and sew through this layer and sleeve only. You will need to fold the seam allowance on the other edge out of the way of the work using the machine basting completed in step 3 as a guide. Fold the cuff into position, pressing the seam allowances down between layers of cuff. Using the machine basting line as a guide, fold the unsecured edge of the cuff to cover the seam allowances and edge- or sink-stitch into position. Sew button to underlap and complete the buttonhole. (7) Fold the yoke, wrong sides facing, to match notches, and stitch into position. Unfold the fabric and press the tuck toward the armhole. Repeat until all tucks are completed. Check the yoke panel against the yoke lining. If completed correctly, the tucked panel will match the lining piece. If desired, you can use the lining pattern piece to cut the main fabric and make the yoke without tuck detailing. (8) Sew darts on front, back, and yoke pieces. Press dart excess toward the side seams.

▶▶ PATTERN TIP

The sleeves from the maxi dress (see page 36) can also be constructed with this design.

⑥

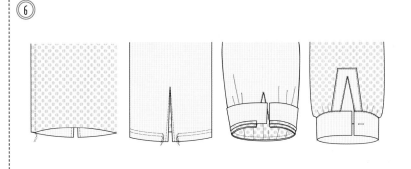

⑦

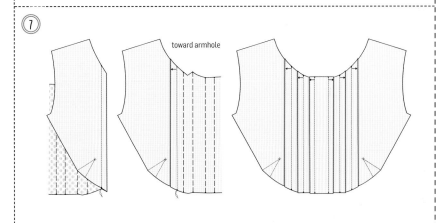

toward armhole

⑧

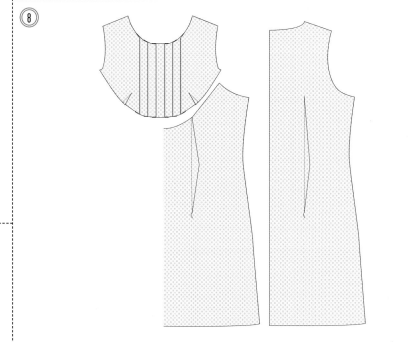

(9) With right sides together, sew yoke to front. (10) Press seam allowances toward the hem. With right sides facing, join side and shoulder seams. (11) Machine the center back seam. Place right sides together, set the machine to its longest stitch and, using a ⅝in (1.5cm) seam allowance, machine baste to the bottom of the zipper opening. Return the machine to its usual stitch setting, make a couple of backstitches, and machine to hem. (12) Press CB seam open and insert zipper using the semi-concealed method detailed on page 176. Unpick the machine basting to release the opening. (13) Turn the garment to the right side and lay the collar to the neckline. Hand baste into position to stop slippage when the facing is attached in the next stage. (14) Lay the facing onto the dress and collar pieces, with right sides facing, thus sandwiching the collar pieces between the yoke section and the yoke lining. Using a ½in (1.2cm) seam allowance, machine through all layers. (15) Under-stitch the seam allowances to the facing only and grade the seam allowances to reduce bulk. Press the facing into position and sew the yoke lining to the yoke through seam allowances only. Alternatively, sink-stitch through the yoke seam. (16) Fold the seam allowances on the back facing and handstitch to zipper and center back seam allowances only. Insert sleeve, stitching through all layers and using the method on page 162. Hem to finish.

9

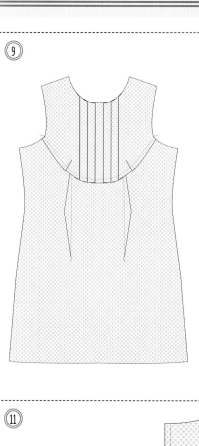

10

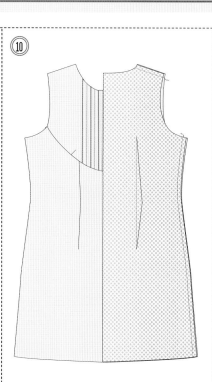

11

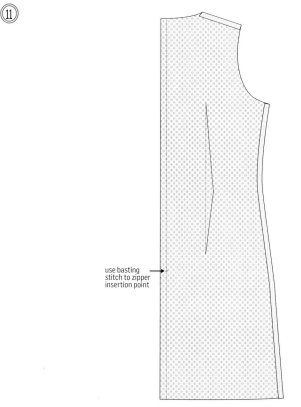

use basting stitch to zipper insertion point

12

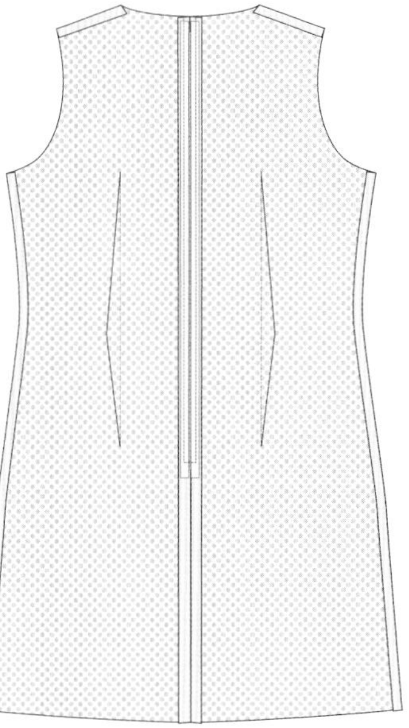

13

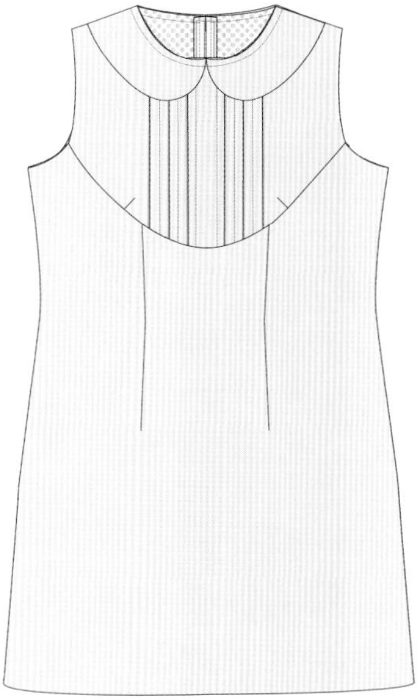

14

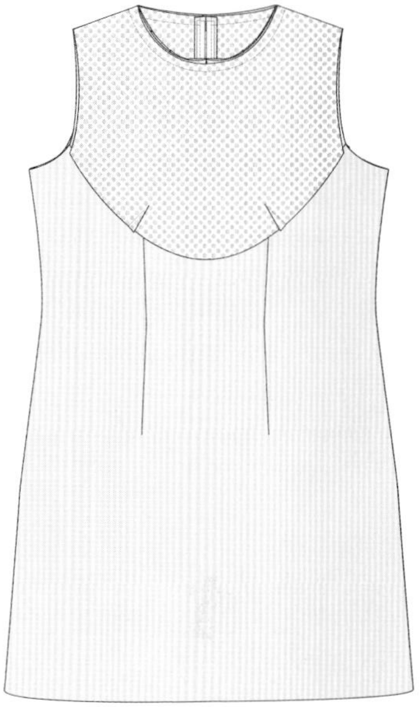

15

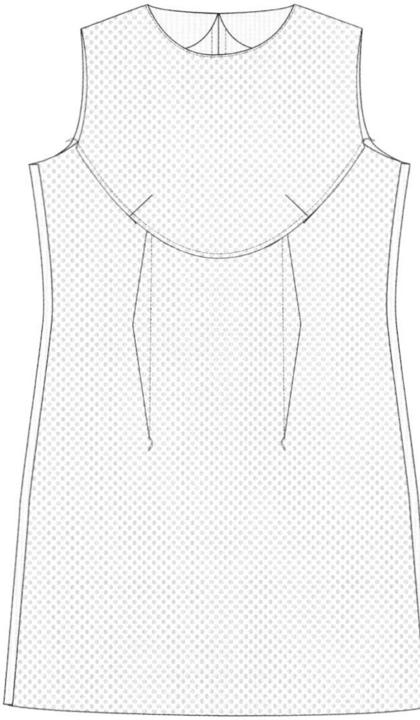

16

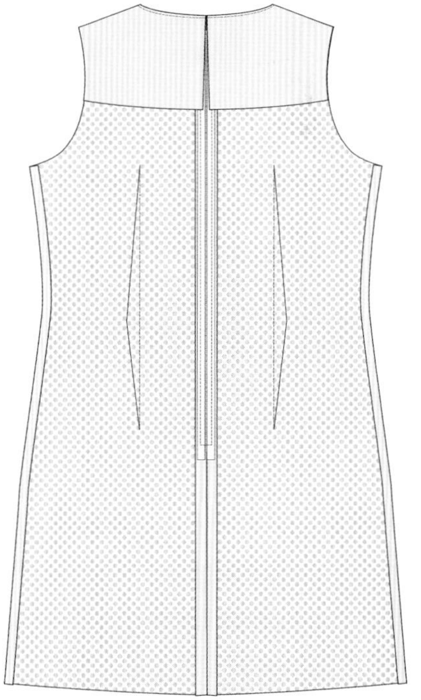

Maxi dress: 1970s

GARMENT SPEC

This dress has gathered detail at the bust. It can be constructed with one of two sleeve options: a short, full sleeve that is gathered into a cuff (sleeve A), or a wrist-length fitted sleeve with a little height at the crown (sleeve B). Suitable for medium-weight fabrics.

Sizes	S (in)	S (cm)	M (in)	M (cm)	L (in)	L (cm)	XL (in)	XL (cm)
Bust at armhole	36 1/4	92	38 3/16	97	40 3/16	102	42 1/8	107
Waist on seam	27 3/16	69	29 1/8	74	31 1/8	79	33 1/16	84
Hem on seam	99 3/8	252.4	101 5/16	257.4	103 5/16	262.4	105 1/4	267.4
Shoulder	4 3/16	10.7	4 5/16	11	4 7/16	11.3	4 9/16	11.6
CB length to hem	55 7/16	140.8	55 11/16	141.4	55 7/8	142	56 1/8	142.6
Zipper length	21 5/8	54.9	21 7/8	55.5	22 1/16	56.1	22 5/16	56.7
Sleeve length ex cuff B	8 7/16	21.45	8 5/8	21.85	8 3/4	22.25	8 15/16	22.65
Sleeve length ex cuff A	10 1/2	26.6	10 5/8	27	10 13/16	27.4	10 15/16	27.8
Cuff width A	1 15/16	5	1 15/16	5	1 15/16	5	1 15/16	5

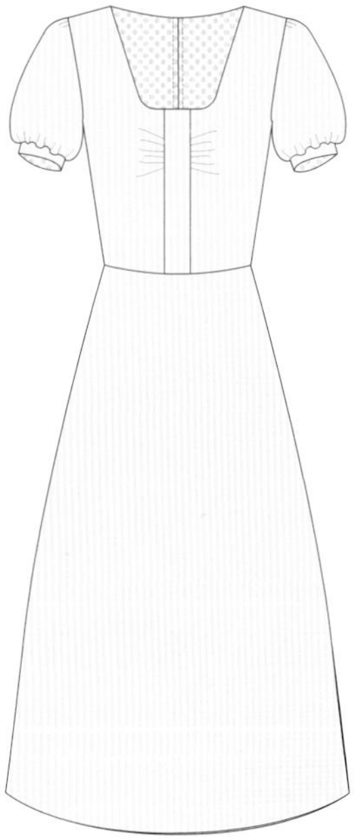

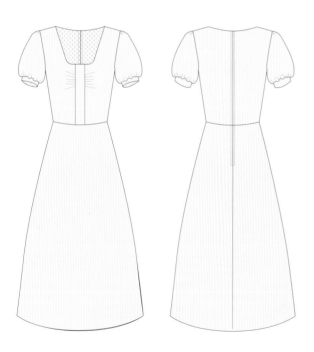

Sleeve A: Front

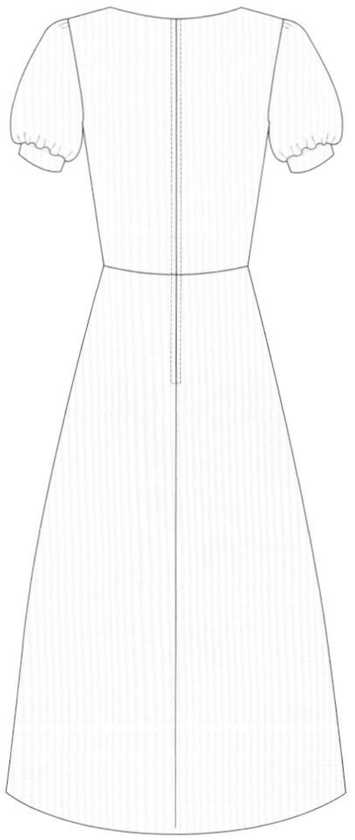

Sleeve A: Back

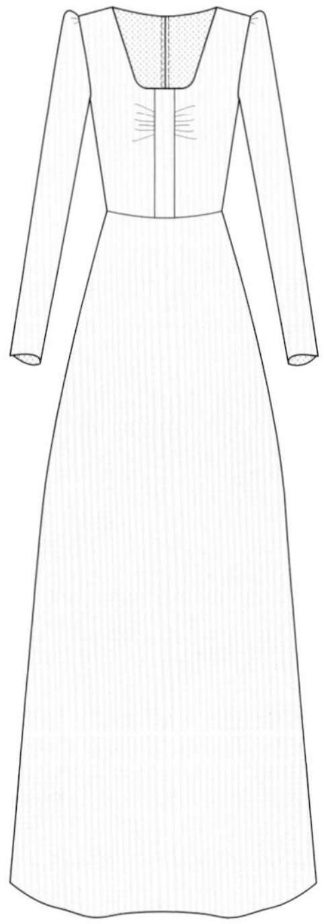

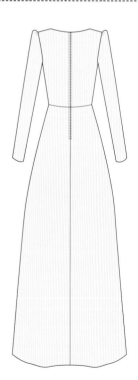

Sleeve B: Front

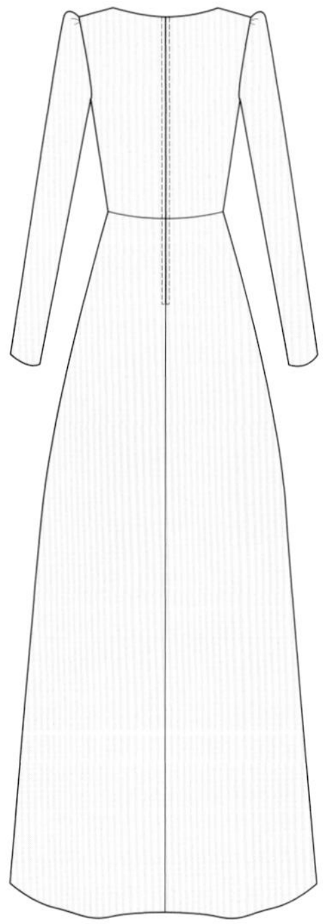

Sleeve B: Back

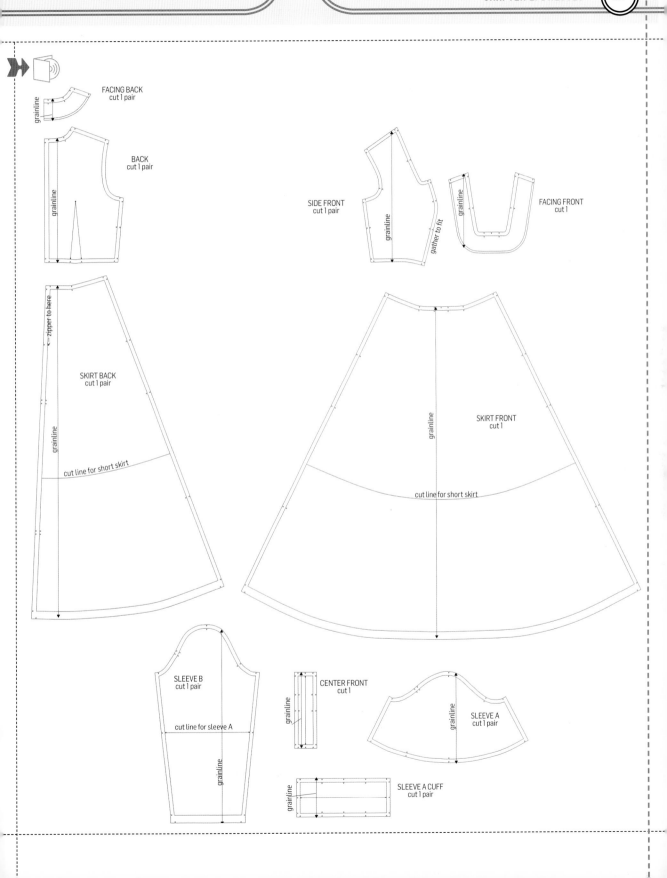

With sleeve A

PATTERN INSTRUCTIONS

(1) Prepare the facing. With right sides together, sew the shoulder seams. Press the seam allowances open and finish the lower edge with overlocking or zigzag stitch.

(2) Prepare the cuff. Set the machine to its longest stitch and sew a line of machine basting ½in (1.2cm) along one of the longest edges. Return the stitch length to its usual setting. Fold the cuff in half widthways with RS facing and stitch the short edge. Then press the seam allowances open.

(3) Prepare the sleeve. With RS together, sew the underarm seam and press the seam allowances open. Set the machine to its longest stitch and sew two lines of gathering stitch along the sleeve hem. Return the settings to the usual stitch length. (4) Join the cuff. Gather stitch to cuff measurement, ensuring that the gathers have been distributed evenly, and place the unbasted edge of the cuff to the sleeve with right sides facing. Stitch into position and press the seam allowances downward. Fold the cuff in half and, using the machine basting as a guide, fold the seam allowance inside to hide all raw edges within folded cuff. Sink- or edge-stitch into place. (5) Set the machine to its longest stitch and make two lines of gathering stitch between notches on side front panels.

(6) Return the machine to its usual stitch length. Gather the side front to match the center front strip, and with right sides together, machine in place.

STYLE VARIATIONS

The sleeve for the previous style (see page 30) will also fit with this garment, which can also be shortened to a knee-length skirt to give a more 1940s feel.

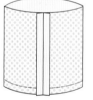

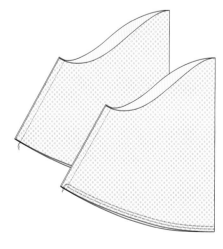

④

⑤

⑥

(7) Join the other side and press the seam allowances toward center front. (8) Sew the back darts, pressing dart excess toward the side seams. (9) With right sides facing, sew the shoulder and side seams, then press the seam allowances open. (10) With right sides together, join waist seam and press seam allowances open. Machine stitch center back seam. Place right sides together, set the machine to its longest stitch and, using a ⅝in (1.5cm) seam allowance, machine baste to the bottom of the zipper opening. (11) Return the machine to its usual setting, make a couple of backstitches to secure the opening, and machine to hem. Press CB seam open and insert zipper using the semi-concealed method on page 176. Unpick the machine basting to release the opening. (12) Turn garment to right side and lay facing to neckline. (13) Machine into position with a ½in (1.2cm) seam allowance. Understitch the seam allowances to the facing only and grade the seam allowances to reduce bulk. Press the facing into position and handstitch to zipper and center back seam allowances only. Insert sleeve, using the method on page 162. Hem to finish.

With sleeve B

To create sleeve B, skip the instruction for cuff construction and insert the sleeve using the tubular method described on page 162. Note that sleeve B has additional height in the crown, which will result in extra fullness. You will need to gather this between the notches as for the tubular method, ensuring that the majority of excess is evenly distributed across the shoulder portion of the sleeve.

⑦

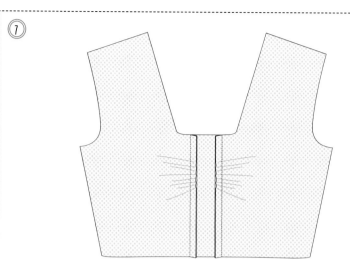

⑧

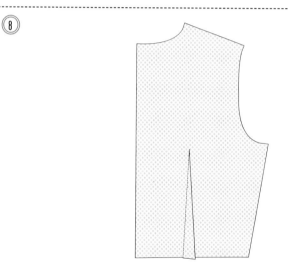

⑨

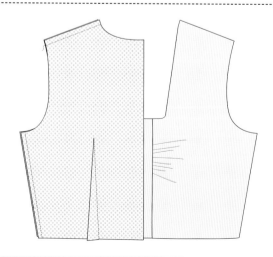

⑩

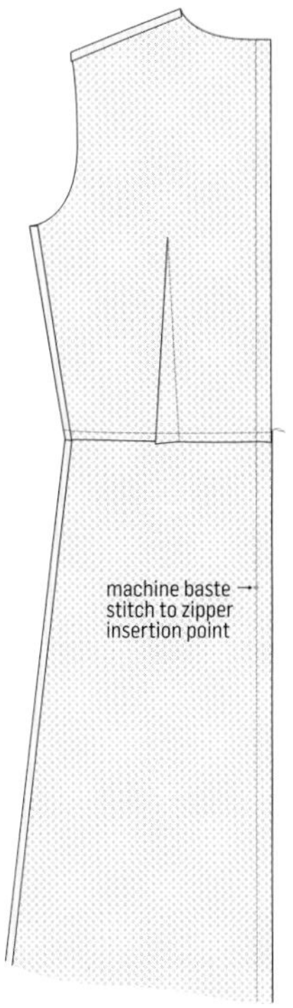

machine baste →
stitch to zipper
insertion point

⑪

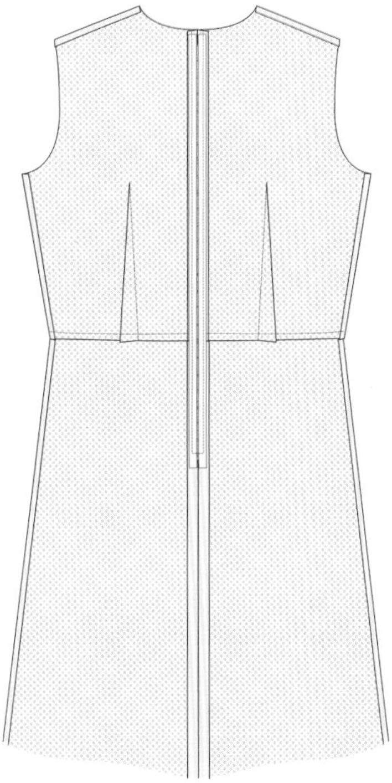

⑫

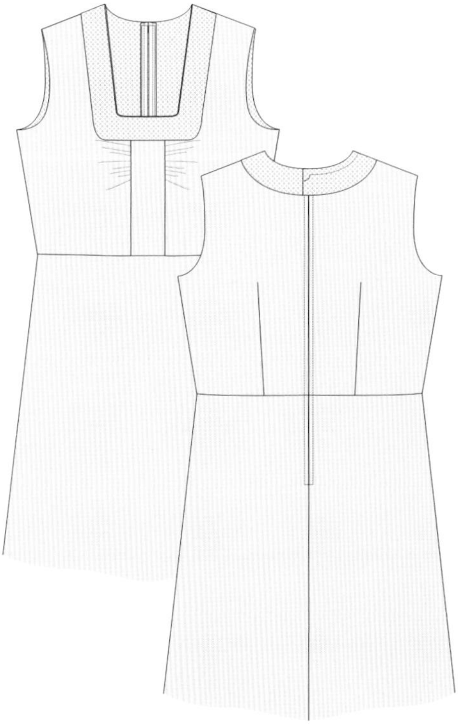

⑬

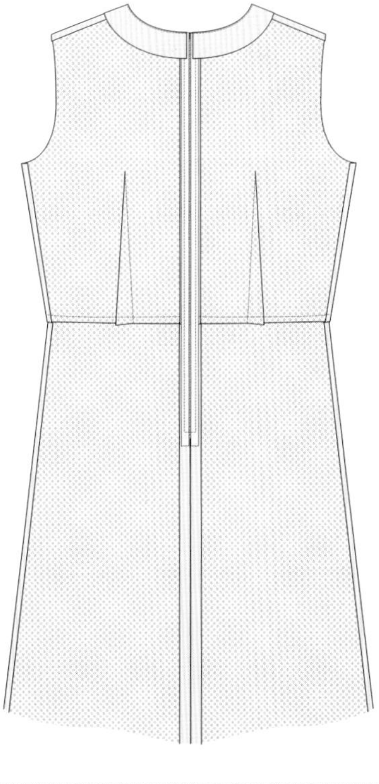

CHAPTER 2
Blouses and detailing

Women first started wearing blouses during the Edwardian era, teaming a high-necked, ornate, lace-trimmed white blouse with full-length, heavy-weight skirts. A distinctive look of this time was the leg-of-mutton sleeve, which was very full at the top of the arm and tight-fitting on the lower half of the arm. As women increasingly entered the workforce during the 20th century, the shirt or blouse made a useful addition to a working wardrobe, being smart, unfussy, and professional-looking. Some shirt styles are functional and unisex, suitable for uniforms and professional outfits; others are made more deliberately feminine with the addition of features such as the demure and girlish Peter Pan collar. In the 1970s, collars were long and winged, and shirts were often close-fitting to contrast with an A-line skirt or flared pants or jeans.

Rozzie shirt. *Eucalyptus*

Buttons: 1920s on

THEN

The 1930s brought about a new type of synthetic material that saw button design reach its most advanced and extravagant state since the eighteenth century.

The button industry was quick to exploit the opportunities that synthetic materials offered. Nicknamed the "material of a thousand uses," Bakelite, invented in 1907, almost completely replaced all other brands of plastics used for buttons; the introduction of Catalin plastic in the 1930s was another step forward. Button designs added a lighthearted touch to fashion design, with novelty styles such as fruit and cigarette packets becoming popular.

A scene in the 1936 film *Modern Times* saw Charlie Chaplin chase around after buttons that were prominently displayed on the backs and bodices of nearby women's dresses in an attempt to tighten them. This aptly captured the decade's fascination with buttons and added to their potential for frivolity.

WHO: The invention of Bakelite and Catalin plastics in the early decades of the twentieth century gave designers the opportunity to make buttons a feature of design, rather than being purely functional.

WHY: Buttons were a great way to display creativity and novelty during wartime, when fabric was in short supply.

VARIATIONS: Studio buttons catered to the collectors' market and were often never worn. Simple, traditional designs are still crucial for functional reasons.

SIMILAR STYLES: N/A

PATTERNS TO MATCH WITH: N/A

NOW

Cardigan. *Orla Kiely*

Style and uses, then and now

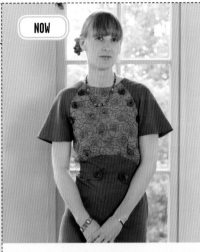

NOW

Button dress. *Decades of Style*

MATERIALS

Then: Wood, cork, Plexiglas, and plastics were all used to make buttons.

Now: Plastic is still used to great effect; some natural materials, including whale ivory, elephant ivory, and tortoiseshell, have been banned.

LENGTH

Then: Elsa Schiaparelli took size to extremes during the 1930s, creating large, ornate buttons resembling brooches.

Now: Dolce & Gabbana continued in this tradition for their 2009 collection, creating beautiful and large shell-like buttons.

STYLE

Then: Buttons could be plain or could be used for display and self-expressive adornment; this impulse continues to give rise to extraordinary examples of the craft.

Now: Buttons remain a great detail that designers can utilize for both functional and fun purposes.

COLORS

Then: Vibrant colors and novelty styles (nicknamed "goofies") were popular, and added interest to all styles of clothing.

Now: All colors are readily available and are often used to punctuate or complement different styles.

MATCHED WITH

Then: The restrictions on fashion implemented by World War II austerity measures meant that buttons offered a way of adding interest to a style. Sewn onto minimalist styles in somber palettes, buttons brought some life to clothes.

Now: The phase for novelty buttons has somewhat passed, but buttons are now often both bright and functional. Seen as essential additions to some styles, buttons are found on a wide variety of clothing in a number of colors and designs.

NOW

Dress. *Family Affairs*

SEWING TIPS

- Match thread to button and use a double thread to provide strength and durability.

- Don't stitch tightly; functional buttons require space for the overlap of fabric.

- After passing the thread through each hole in the button, bring the needle out between button and garment and wrap the thread around the anchored strands two or three times to tighten the stitches and create a shank.

The Peter Pan collar: 1920s on

Peter Pan collars have added simple yet desirable design detail to costumes, dresses, and shirts since the 1800s, and continue to be revived to fit each new fashion era.

London's Victoria & Albert Museum displays a child's cloak featuring a layered and scalloped Peter Pan collar dating back to the 1830s, alongside a 1950s skirt suit and 1960s Mary Quant mod dress both boasting designs that illustrate the evolution of this style. However, it was the costume worn by actress Maude Adams in the first American stage production of J. M. Barrie's play *Peter and Wendy* that gave the detail its name.

Previously, this rounded collar, worn separately from the rest of the outfit so it could be cleaned more often, was synonymous with children's uniforms such as Quaker dress, the *Little Lord Fauntleroy* boys, and the schoolgirl in Colette's 1900 novel *Claudine à l'école*. Although it enjoyed a grown-up makeover over the course of the twentieth century, it is the demure schoolgirl look that is popular again today, with Peter Pan–collar shirts being worn with preppy jumpers and skirts and adorning simple dresses.

WHO: Made fashionable by Maude Adams's costume in the first U.S. stage production of J. M. Barrie's play *Peter and Wendy*.

WHY: Simple and versatile design detail.

VARIATIONS: Scalloped collars and flat pointed styles.

SIMILAR STYLES: Rever collar, page 48; dog-eared collar, page 50

PATTERNS TO MATCH WITH: Mini dress, page 30; blouse, page 54

Shirt dress. *Aubin & Wills*

Style and uses, then and now

FABRIC

Then: In the 1800s and early 1900s, starched cotton was popular for the detachable Peter Pan collar. For formal wear, such as wedding dresses in the 1930s and 1940s, silk was the preferred material.

Now: Cotton, polyester, and velvet are favored for the style, with detachable metal and beaded accessories also taking the place of the traditional fabric Peter Pan collar.

LENGTH

Then: Flat and wide collars were used to decorate costumes and uniforms in the 1880s and 1890s, while smaller, rounded collars came into fashion during the Midcentury.

Now: Small, rounded collars are enjoying renewed popularity in mainstream fashion stores, while longer and wider styles have been championed on the fashion catwalks.

STYLE

Then: At the beginning of the twentieth century, the Peter Pan collar was worn wide and flat, sometimes with frill and lace detail, on children's uniforms and women's occasion wear. The style was often beaded on midcentury cocktail dresses, and was stripped back to its simpler form for the 1960s mod look.

Now: Today, small, rounded collars adorn dresses and shirts, while detachable collars are often printed with motifs, made from vintage floral material, or crafted from metals and beads to form alternative accessories.

COLORS

Then: White, starched collars were popular for costumes, uniforms, and occasion wear in the detail's early days, while brighter colors and contrasting black or white styles became fashionable during the midcentury era.

Now: Contrasting black or white collars have been revived by current designers and fashion icons such as Alexa Chung and Zooey Deschanel, while other monochrome color combinations and vibrant vintage prints are also in style.

MATCHED WITH

Then: Children's uniforms, such as short pants, school dresses, and costumes, followed by long wedding dresses in the 1930s and 40s and cocktail dress styles in the Midcentury era.

Now: Most commonly added as a design detail to shift dresses, often sleeveless or with bell sleeves, or to crisp cotton or sheer shirts.

SEWING TIPS

- To create a Peter Pan collar that doesn't sag, use interfacing to give your collar body.

- If you are using a fusible interfacing, fuse the undercollar.

- It is often easier to fuse fabric prior to cutting out to reduce stretch and distortion.

- Use another layer of translucent fabric as the interfacing for a sheer collar. This will provide body without spoiling the effect of the fabric.

NOW

Shift top with Peter Pan collar. *Primark*

The rever collar: 1950s

THEN

A traditional-looking four-pointed collar style that is instantly recognizable, the rever collar has been used in the construction of shirts and blouses since the early 1900s. Often seen on the wide lapels of shirts, jackets, and coats, the front neckline turns back or folds over to create the effect. This is a unisex style that is often sported on an open-necked shirt.

Thought of as a simple, nonfussy, functional design, the rever collar blouse came into its own in the hands of Claire McCardell, the American designer who made elegant daywear that was affordable and available off-the-rack. She used unpretentious fabrics and avoided applied decoration and ornamental devices. In the 1950s, she introduced the rever collar shirtwaist dress with circular skirts in bold colors, which became a sought-after style of the time.

WHO: Easy-to-wear daywear was brought into the fashion spotlight by Claire McCardell.

WHY: Can be made from readily available and cost-effective fabrics.

VARIATIONS: Traditional pointed collars offer a similar, if slightly more tailored, approach.

SIMILAR STYLES: Peter Pan collar, page 46; dog-eared collar, page 50

PATTERNS TO MATCH WITH: Blouse, page 54; box-pleated skirt, page 66; wide-legged pants, page 82

NOW

Striped shirt. *Urban Outfitters*

Style and uses, then and now

FABRIC

Then: Cotton was the most popular fabric, as it was accessible and easy to work with. Muslin was also an option. Gingham was also used, especially through the late 1950s rockabilly era.

Now: Cotton is still a popular choice; poplin is sometimes used, and organic cotton is becoming more readily available. Blended pinpoint cottons offer extra breathability during summer months.

LENGTH

Then: Short rever collars were seen on boxy, short-sleeved blouses.

Now: Collar lengths are still short on blouses, with boxy styles often a summer favorite.

STYLE

Then: A style often donned by rockabilly teenagers, the rever blouse had its fashion moment during the 1950s. The style also appealed to those in a more professional environment, but was generally worn in plain fabrics.

Now: Seeking to convey a "sexy secretary" look, Prada has used the rever collar blouse to great effect in recent collections.

COLORS

Then: This style supports a variety of hues. Yellows, baby pinks, and light blues were popular in the 1950s, while ivory offered a more sophisticated option.

Now: Prints are currently a fashion favorite, while vibrant tones add to the laid-back look a rever collar blouse can achieve.

MATCHED WITH

Then: The 1950s look was completed with a poodle, circle skirt, ankle socks, belts, and Mary Jane shoes.

Now: Tuck a rever-collar blouse into a pencil skirt to add movement to a silhouette.

NOW

Blazers with rever collar. *Betty Barclay*

SEWING TIPS

- Miter seam allowances to reduce bulk and make turning easier.

- Push the corners out carefully and do not be tempted to use the sharp points of your scissors to turn out a corner.

- Do not over-press a turned-out collar as this can result in the profile edges of the seam allowance showing through and spoiling the appearance.

The dog-eared collar: 1970s

THEN

A collar frames the face and draws attention to it, so it is without doubt one of the most important details on any shirt or blouse. The dog-eared collar is an oversized-style collar, so named because the points on the collar were thought to resemble a floppy-eared dog. Popular in the 1970s, the style was often seen on button-front, yoked, puff-sleeve blouses. Slit V-necklines were also popular.

Busy prints were used to great effect in this era, and the elongated style of the dog-eared collar added to the desirable long and lean silhouette of the decade.

WHO: Yves Saint Laurent adapted masculine tailoring for womenswear, including dog-eared collar styles.

WHY: This style of long collar accompanied the popularity of the long, svelte silhouette that came into play during the 1970s.

VARIATIONS: More traditional pointed collars were also used to great effect during this period.

SIMILAR STYLES: Peter Pan collar, page 46; rever collar, page 48

PATTERNS TO MATCH WITH: Blouse, page 54; box-pleated skirt, page 66; wide-legged pants, page 82

NOW

Dog-eared collar dress. *Old Age Vintage*

NOW

Apple print dog-eared collar dress. *Old Age Vintage*

Style and uses, then and now

FABRIC

Then: Synthetic fabrics were often used, although natural fibers were also popular. Cotton and courtelle jersey were other popular choices, and by the late 1970s fabrics such as viscose, polyester, and rayon were common.

Now: Synthetic fabrics are often used today, with the collar interfacing matching the weight of the shirt or blouse.

LENGTH

Then: Dog-eared collars reached their extremes in length during the 1970s; a 7-inch (17.5cm) length was not unusual.

Now: The popular length is a more conservative 5 to 6 inches (12.5 to 16.25cm).

STYLE

Then: Worn by fashion-forward ladies, the dog-eared collar shirt signaled 1970s-style liberation and independence, as such shirts were regularly teamed with pants.

Now: This collar was very much a 1970s trend. Marc Jacobs gave the look a modern twist in the 2010s, and featured variations of the style in his designs.

COLORS

Then: Creamy-white tones were paired with burnt-orange sweater vests. Vibrant patterns played a part, and it was around this era that people really started to experiment with more exotic hues.

Now: This type of collar is often seen on styles with a retro flavor. Purple, mustard, red, and traditional cream tones all work well with the dog-eared collar.

MATCHED WITH:

Then: Worn under sweater vests, with jeans, platform shoes, or flared pants, the dog-eared collar enhanced the elongated silhouette of the era.

Now: The dog-eared collar has been spotted worn under pinafore dresses and with flared pants for a retro effect.

SEWING TIPS

- Turning out a dog-eared style can be tricky: a pressing template can prove invaluable in helping to turn a neat collar. Trace a copy of the collar pattern, without seam allowances, onto cardboard and insert into the turned-out collar pieces to press.

- Using contrasting fabrics or varying the grain positioning on a patterned fabric can add an extra element to this simple design.

Dog-eared collar. (Model's own)

Western cowgirl blouse. *H Bar C*

Shirt cuffs: 1970s

The cuff on a shirt or blouse has two main purposes: to be functional, and to be an attractive design feature, giving a smart finish to a sleeve. The 1970s saw a rise in blouses with wide wrist cuffs in female tailoring.

To give it emphasis, the cuff is often cut on a different grain or in a contrast fabric. A wide cuff or a double cuff is usually seen on blouses made from lightweight fabrics to balance the design.

Feminine features such as ruffles, ties, or embroidered decorations made sure the cuff made its mark on 1970s-era blouses.

WHO: A popular style that stems from Yves Saint Laurent's appropriation of masculine tailoring for womenswear.

WHY: As pants and jeans reached the height of their popularity in the 1970s, the wide-cuff blouse was the perfect partner for these styles.

VARIATIONS: Turn-up cuffs offer a sporty edge, while rolled-up cuffs give shirts a casual look.

SIMILAR STYLES: N/A

PATTERNS TO MATCH WITH: Blouse, page 54

NOW

Puff-sleeve shirt. (Model's own)

Style and uses, then and now

FABRIC

Then: Cotton and silk were often used, while thicker types of polyester were also popular.

Now: Thin, lightweight cotton is still the preferred fabric choice, with polyester, satin, and silk also often used.

LENGTH

Then: The beginning of the 1970s saw the double cuff gain in popularity, with the blouson style ever popular.

Now: After the rise of the three-quarter-length sleeve in the 1990s, the cuff has returned to a more traditional shirt-like length.

STYLE

Then: Worn by women who wanted to stay ahead of the trends, the double-cuff shirts and blouses of the 1970s were thought of as fashion-forward with a masculine twist.

Now: With button-fastening cuffs making a great partner to a tailored suit, women still often wear cuffed blouses in the workplace.

COLORS

Then: The cuffs' color matched the blouse color, with popular hues being mustard yellow, orange, red, and green.

Now: The colors used for blouses and shirts shift whenever trends change. With vintage fashion currently at the forefront, orange tones are still often seen. More traditional creams and whites are also worn.

MATCHED WITH

Then: Worn under sweater vests and teamed with maxi skirts, flared jeans, and tailored pants, double-cuff blouses and shirts added a chic, tailored element to many looks.

Now: A versatile style that can be worn from day to night and with a variety of different options, the cuffed blouse maintains an air of elegance. Balance out a blouson style by teaming it with fitted pants or a pencil skirt.

NOW

Shirt with ruffled cuffs. *Very.co.uk*

NOW

Imogen blouse. *Matilda & Quinn*

SEWING TIPS

- Use interlining or fusible interfacing to give body and support to a cuff, but make sure you choose one that isn't too stiff.

- It is usually easier to attach a cuff to a sleeve before the sleeve is attached to the garment. As a rule of thumb, complete the cuff first on a tubed sleeve; for garments with the underarm and side seam constructed in one, attach the cuff at a later stage.

Blouse: 1920s / 1940s / 1970s

GARMENT SPEC

This blouse has a full bishop sleeve and a choice of a rounded or a dog-eared collar. This design is suitable for light- and medium-weight fabrics.

STYLE VARIATIONS

You could construct this blouse using waist darts to give a fitted look, or without waist darts for a more relaxed shape. Consider applying a shaped patch pocket too.

Front: dog-eared collar without waist shaping

Back: dog-eared collar without waist shaping

Front: round collar with waist shaping

Back: round collar with waist shaping

Sizes	S (in)	S (cm)	M (in)	M (cm)	L (in)	L (cm)	XL (in)	XL (cm)
Bust at armhole	$35\frac{11}{16}$	90.6	$37\frac{5}{8}$	95.6	$39\frac{5}{8}$	100.6	$41\frac{9}{16}$	105.6
Waist $7\frac{1}{16}$in (18cm) below armhole	$31\frac{5}{16}$	79.5	$33\frac{1}{4}$	84.5	$35\frac{1}{4}$	89.5	$37\frac{3}{16}$	94.5
Hem on seam	$37\frac{1}{16}$	94.2	$39\frac{1}{16}$	99.2	41	104.2	43	109.2
Shoulder	$4\frac{15}{16}$	12.5	$5\frac{1}{16}$	12.8	$5\frac{3}{16}$	13.1	$5\frac{1}{4}$	13.4
CB length to hem	$23\frac{3}{4}$	60.4	24	61	$24\frac{1}{4}$	61.6	$24\frac{1}{2}$	62.2
Back neck on seam	$5\frac{7}{8}$	14.9	$6\frac{1}{8}$	15.5	$6\frac{5}{16}$	16.1	$6\frac{9}{16}$	16.7
Front neck on seam	$4\frac{11}{16}$	11.9	$4\frac{15}{16}$	12.5	$5\frac{3}{16}$	13.1	$5\frac{3}{8}$	13.7
Bicep	14	35.5	$14\frac{3}{4}$	37.5	$15\frac{9}{16}$	39.5	$5\frac{3}{8}$	41.5
Cuff width	$19\frac{3}{4}$	50.2	$20\frac{3}{16}$	51.2	$20\frac{9}{16}$	52.2	$20\frac{15}{16}$	53.2

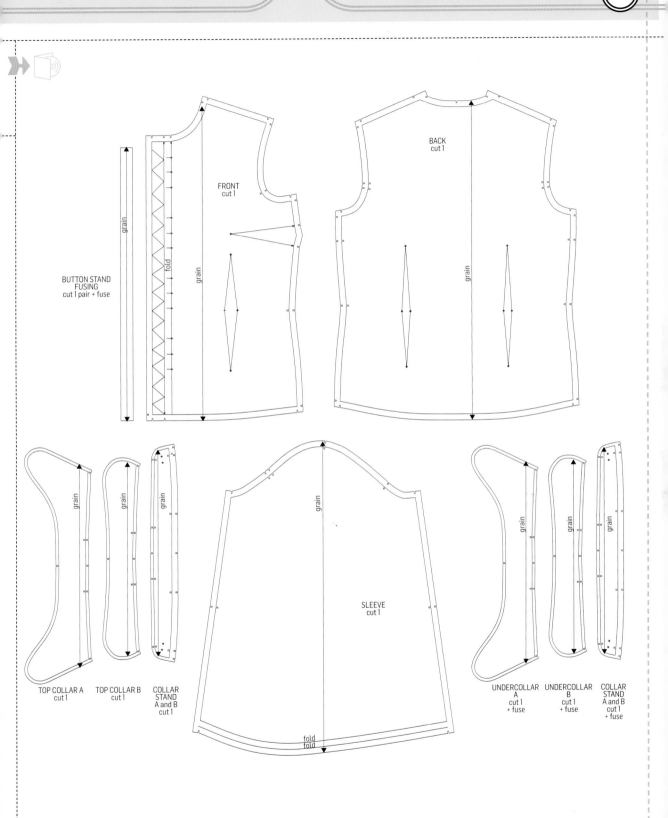

PATTERN INSTRUCTIONS

(1) To prepare the collar, fuse the under-collar and 1 collar stand. With right sides together, and using a ¼in (6mm) seam allowance, sew the top collar and under-collar along the curved edge. Turn out the collar, using a cardboard template to achieve a smooth profile edge, and press. Topstitch the collar approximately ¾6in (5mm) from the edge. Set the machine to its longest stitch and make a line of machine basting along the bottom edge of the fused collar stand ½in (1.2cm) from the bottom edge. With RS together, lay the turned-out collar piece onto the unfused collar stand, then place the fused stand on top, with wrong sides uppermost. Sew through all layers using ¼in (6mm) seam allowances, starting and stopping the stitching level with the machine basting completed at the previous stage. Turn the collar to RS and carefully press using a cardboard template if desired. Fold and press the basted seam allowance upward into the collar and set aside. **(2)** Press the interlining into position and sew darts on the front and back body pieces. **(3)** Using the first notch as a guide, press ½in (1.2cm) seam allowance to wrong side and sew a line of stitching ¾6in (5mm) from the folded edge. Using the second notch as a guide, fold and press the button stand into position and sew a line of stitching ¾6in (5mm) from the edge. **(4)** Complete the buttonholes at center front and on the collar stand.

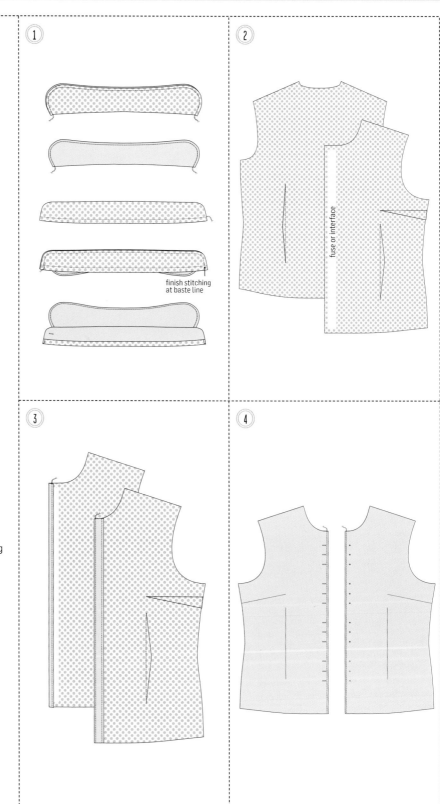

finish stitching at baste line

fuse or interface

(5) With right sides facing, sew the shoulder and side seams. Press the seam allowances open. **(6)** To attach the collar, turn the garment to RS and lay the unfolded edge of the collar stand to the neckline. Stitch in place using a ½in (1.2cm) seam allowance. Fold the collar in position, pushing seam allowances upward between collar stand pieces, and cover with the folded edge of the button stand. Edge- or sink-stitch into place and complete a line of topstitching ³⁄₁₆in (5mm) from the edge. **(7)** Fold the sleeve in half with RS facing and sew the underarm seam. Press the seam allowances open. **(8)** Double-turn the sleeve hem to make a channel for the elastic, leaving a gap to thread the elastic through. Insert the elastic and finish stitching. Insert the sleeve into the armhole using the method described on page 162 and finish the hem.

⑤

⑥

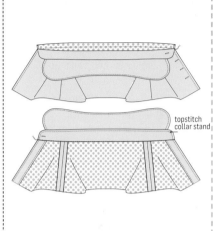

topstitch collar stand

⑦

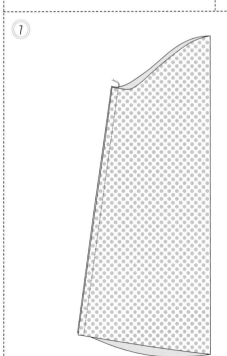

⑧

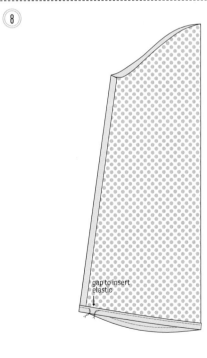

gap to insert elastic

CHAPTER 3
Skirts

Skirt shapes and lengths generally followed dress styles and silhouettes in the twentieth century, although skirts were often considered appropriate for more casual occasions and daywear. Women in the 1930s and 1940s often wore skirt suits in practical, hardwearing fabrics such as tweed. As women's participation in sports became more commonplace, short pleated skirts were adopted for activities such as tennis. The 1950s introduced new silhouettes: the circle skirt supported on layers of petticoats is a key look of the decade, while the elegant pencil skirt, smart enough for work and glamorous enough for eveningwear, is still a popular style. The mini-skirt of the 1960s became an iconic fashion item that symbolized the youthful rebellion of that era, while mid-calf and maxi skirts are styles that have been revived in recent years.

Pencil skirt.
Internacionale

The pencil skirt: 1950s

The pencil skirt was created to accentuate a woman's natural curves, and is cut slim, straight, and narrow. Pencil skirts usually fall to, or just below, the knee and often have a slit in the back or side so that the wearer can walk more easily. Pencil skirts are extremely versatile and quickly became popular office wear in the early 1950s, although their classic style means they can also be dressed down with different-colored tights, shoes, and accessories for a more casual look.

WHO: French designer, Christian Dior, introduced the classic pencil skirt.

WHY: Pencil skirts were designed to accentuate the natural curves of a woman's body, and catered to the postwar desire for new feminine fashions.

SIMILAR STYLES: Box-pleated skirt, page 66

PATTERNS TO MATCH WITH: Blouse, page 54

Metallic dogtooth pencil skirt. *M&co*

Style and uses, then and now

FABRIC

Then: Pencil skirts were often made from linen, cotton, wool, tweed, silk, and rayon.

Now: Can be made from a huge variety of fabrics: lightweight wool or cotton accentuate the curves, yet still have some give and allow for movement and comfort.

LENGTH

Then: Pencil skirts were best known for being knee-length or up to 2 inches (5cm) below the knee.

Now: Modern pencil skirts generally conform to knee-length styles.

STYLE

Then: Pencil skirts were simple and classic, around knee-length and plain in color.

Now: Pencil skirts today are similar in style, but can be modernized with wide waistbands and finishes such as lace and bows.

COLORS

Then: Pencil skirts were restricted to the fabric colors available at the time. When pencil skirts emerged as office wear they were popular in darker colors and shades, such as black and gray.

Now: Modern pencil skirts are available in a huge variety of colors and prints.

MATCHED WITH

Then: Pencil skirts in the 1960s were worn with fitted blouses, soft sweaters, jackets, or tunics—clothing with nipped-in waists that accentuated a woman's curves. Corsets, once abandoned, regained popularity to enhance the pencil-skirt shape. High heels and stockings were also a popular match with pencil skirts.

Now: To conform to a retro style, wear with fishnet stockings, heels, a shrunken jacket or cropped cardigan, a string of pearls or a brooch. A basic principle of wearing a pencil skirt is to keep it unadorned, so no belts, pockets, or pleats. Short-length ankle boots are also a fashionable footwear addition to complement the pencil-skirt style.

SEWING TIPS

- The key to a successful pencil skirt is accurate measurements for the top, waist, bottom, and length.

- Source a relatively strong fabric with some stretch. If you would prefer not to fuss with a zipper and darts, use jersey or spandex.

NOW

Scuba pencil skirt. *Penneys (Ireland)*

The circle skirt: 1950s

"instant" SKIRT
Paper pattern
is all one piece;
pin to fabric
and cut complete
skirt instantly

THEN

Circle skirts became popular in the 1950s. Following World War II, dress restrictions were lifted, hemlines dropped, and skirts became fuller as part of Christian Dior's New Look.

Circle skirts are named after their construction; they are usually made from a large circular piece of fabric with a cutout in the center for the waist (although cheaper circle skirts are cut in sections to make one or more circles). The circular construction of the style accentuates the feminine shape and hangs smoothly from the waist without darts, pleats, or gathers. Petticoats can be worn underneath to achieve the full effect and to make more of a distinction between the narrow waist and the full skirt.

Although there were different varieties of the circle skirt available in the 1950s, poodle skirts are the best-known; these are made from wool felt and decorated with appliqués, embroidery, and other embellishments. The rise in popularity of the circle skirt coincided with the emergence of rock 'n' roll music, and the flowing fullness of the circle skirt allowed its wearer to twirl and dance freely and energetically to the music.

WHO: The full shape of the circle skirt came about as part of Christian Dior's New Look; Juli Lynne Charlot is credited as being the original designer of the poodle skirt.

WHY: Because of its simple shape, the circle skirt is easy to make and embellish. The full skirt shape also made it suitable for dancing to energetic rock 'n' roll music.

VARIATIONS: Variations include the poodle skirt, conversation skirt, Mexican circle skirt, three-quarter circle skirt, and semicircle skirt.

SIMILAR STYLES: Prom dress, page 26

PATTERNS TO MATCH WITH: Maxi dress, page 36; 1940s slip, page 120; bustier, page 124

NOW

Cowburn skirt. *Hobbs*

NOW

Pleated circle skirt. *Tatyana Khomyakova for Bettie Page*

Style and uses, then and now

FABRIC

Then: Poodle skirts were made from wool felt and decorated with felt appliqués, while more formal skirts were made from lighter fabrics such as silk, muslin, or cotton.

Now: All manner of fabrics can be used to create a circle skirt. Lightweight cottons allow for more flow, while polyester or poly blends can result in a relatively wrinkle-free skirt. If you are a beginner sewer, avoid using stretchy or satiny fabrics, as they are harder to work with.

LENGTH

Then: Typical lengths varied from below-knee to mid-calf.

Now: Retro-style skirts are similar lengths today, but circle skirts are often worn higher, typically around knee-length or above-the-knee.

STYLE

Then: Poodle skirts decorated with appliqué embellishments were the most popular style in the 1950s and were worn with or without a petticoat.

Now: Circle skirts vary more in terms of fabrics and lengths. Different cuts, such as the semicircle skirt, are also available.

COLORS

Then: Poodle skirts were typically made in solid bold colors, often pink and powder blue. Mexican circle skirts were made from bright eye-catching fabrics or were handpainted in bright colors and trimmed with sequins.

Now: The basic circle-skirt design can support a wide variety of colors and patterns. Use solid colurs with appliqué finishes for a more retro look, or bright floral, geometric, or plaid prints for a bolder statement.

MATCHED WITH

Then: Teenage girls in the 1950s wore their poodle skirts with tight-fitting sweaters or short-sleeved blouses, bobby socks, and saddle or white lace-up canvas shoes. A ruffled petticoat or slip was also worn under the skirt to make it stand out fully. Long hair was tied up into a ponytail or a sheer scarf was worn like a hairband.

Now: Circle skirts with wide waistbands are best worn with a loose-fitting blouse, while circle skirts with narrower waistbands look best balanced with a more fitted top such as a camisole, T-shirt, blouse, or sweater. For a more retro look, pair with a cinch belt, a Peter Pan blouse, and a pair of Oxfords.

SEWING TIPS

- If you want more body in a skirt, consider a one-and-a-half circle, which involves gathering one circle at the back and then half at the front. Just add another layer of fabric to the pattern. The easiest thing to do with the waist is to fold it over and insert elastic. A more sophisticated approach is to make a separate casing and sew this onto your skirt, then thread elastic through the casing. Use a band and trouser hooks for a more professional look.

NOW

Circle skirt. *Molly-Made, With Love*

The pleated skirt: 1950s / 1960s

THEN

Pleated skirts can include pleats of various sorts (described below) to add fullness from the waist or hips, or to allow freedom of movement at the hem. While box-pleated skirts in particular were seen in the 1930s, pleated skirts generally came into popular fashion in the 1950s, being complementary to the tailored look of the time. This particularly suited the "preppy" look, which favored tidiness and grooming, and neat pleats were set on the hip and worn with fitted short-sleeved blouses. One famous example of the pleated skirt style is the cheerleading uniform, which developed in the 1960s, complete with its short pleated cotton skirt that allowed for easy movement.

There are various types of pleats that can be used to style a skirt. Accordion pleats are a series of narrow, evenly spaced, parallel pleats; box pleats are double pleats with fabric folded under at each side; knife pleats are sharply creased narrow pleats, usually one of a series folded in the same direction; inverted pleats are reverse box pleats, with the flat fold turned in; and kick pleats are inverted pleats extended upward from the hemline at the back of a narrow skirt, allowing freedom when walking.

WHO: N/A (although the recent revival of pleated skirts is credited as being championed by Miuccia Prada).

WHY: Pleated skirts add fullness from the waist or hips and allow more freedom of movement, which makes them both feminine and suitable for activities such as tennis and cheerleading.

VARIATIONS: There are numerous variations according to the type of pleat, including accordion, box, knife, inverted, and kick pleats.

SIMILAR STYLES: Prom dress, page 26

PATTERNS TO MATCH WITH: Prom dress, page 26; box-pleated skirt, page 66

NOW

NOW

Pleated midi skirt. *House of Fraser*

Pleated maxi skirt. *Goldie London*

Style and uses, then and now

FABRIC

Then: In the 1950s, pleated skirts were often made from polyester. Wool or synthetic acrylics were also used.

Now: Pleated skirts are available in a huge variety of fabrics, from cotton through to leather. Popular pleated styles available today are often made from softer fabrics such as georgette and polyester, which achieve a feminine, "swishing" effect and help to avoid bulk around the hips.

LENGTH

Then: In the 1950s, hemlines were to the knee or just below. Cheerleading pleated skirts in the 1960s were knee-length or just above.

Now: Pleated skirts are available in all different lengths today, from mid-thigh to ankle, although most tend to be knee- or mid-calf-length. Another popular style is a double-layer ankle-length skirt, with a short straight skirt below and a pleated chiffon layer over the top.

STYLE

Then: Worn as part of the preppie teen look in the 1950s, these skirts were knee-length and featured neat pleats.

Now: Today styles are generally more flowing and vary in length. They often incorporate different layers and fabrics.

COLORS

Then: Pleated skirts in the 1950s tended to be available in a range of block colors or in plaid patterns.

Now: Pleated skirts today are available in a huge variety of colors and prints, although when it comes to pleats, primary colors work best.

MATCHED WITH

Then: In the 1950s and 1960s, pleated skirts were matched with chic silk blouses for the work week and soft, slouchy sweaters for a more casual look.

Now: Wearing pleats can add volume, so choose a body-conscious top with a little cling to it—this will contrast with the fullness of the skirt. Most shirts are suitable to wear with pleated skirts, but don't overdo it with patterns. Accents that add volume and accentuate the pleats include a repetitive-motif necklace, large, eye-catching earrings, or a chunky cuff bracelet. Pleated skirts also look good paired with strappy platforms or heels and a clutch.

NOW

Mid-calf pleated skirt. *Viyella*

NOW

Pleated mini-skirt. *Olive Boutique*

SEWING TIPS

- Don't cut fabric lengthwise as it will not drape as well; always cut your fabric horizontally or across the grain.

- It can be difficult to hem a pleated skirt once the pleats have been pressed in—hem once your skirt pieces have been joined together at the side seams and before pleating.

Box-pleated skirt: 1950s

GARMENT SPEC

This simple fitted skirt has three kick pleats set into panels to add flare and ease of movement at the hem. This design is particularly suitable for woolens, but could be made in most medium-weight fabrics.

Sizes	S (in)	S (cm)	M (in)	M (cm)	L (in)	L (cm)	XL (in)	XL (cm)
Bust at armhole	25¹⁄₁₆	63.6	27	68.6	29	73.6	30¹⁵⁄₁₆	78.6
Waist 7¹⁄₁₆in (18cm) below armhole	35⁷⁄₁₆	90	37⅜	95	39⅜	100	41⁵⁄₁₆	105
Hem on seam	35	101.3	40	101.6	40⅛	101.9	40¼	102.2
Shoulder	25³⁄₁₆	63.9	25⅜	64.5	25⅝	65.1	25⅞	65.7
CB length to hem	1³⁄₁₆	3	1³⁄₁₆	3	1³⁄₁₆	3	1³⁄₁₆	3

Front

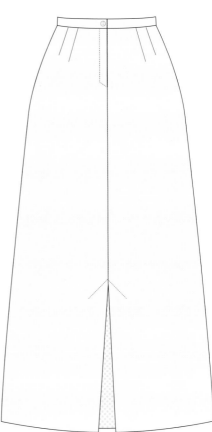

Back

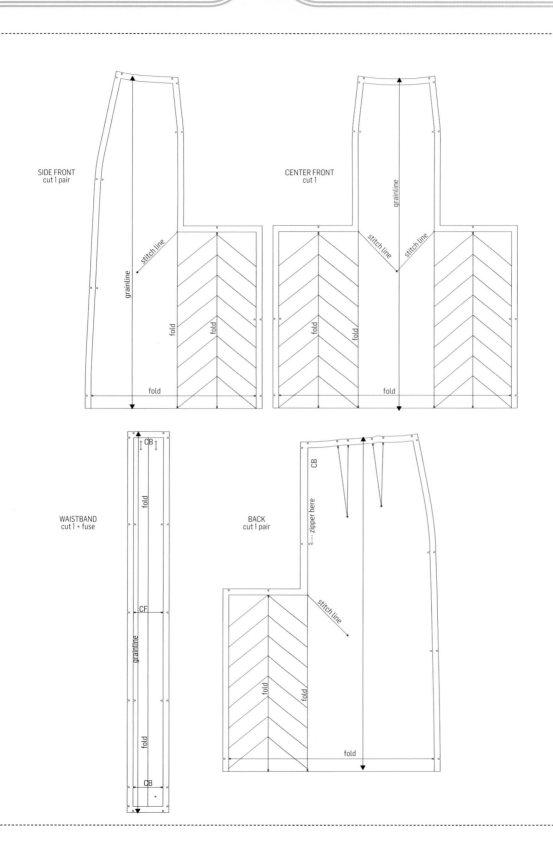

SIDE FRONT
cut 1 pair

CENTER FRONT
cut 1

WAISTBAND
cut 1 + fuse

BACK
cut 1 pair

PATTERN INSTRUCTIONS

(1) First prepare the waistband. Fuse the waistband piece and set the machine to its biggest stitch in order to complete a line of machine basting ½in (1.2cm) from one long edge. Return the machine to its usual stitch settings before continuing. Fold the waistband in half and stitch along the short edge. Sew the underlap along the short edge, pivot at the corner, and sew to the center back notch. Clip the seam allowance close to the stitch line. Miter the corners and turn the waistband to the right side, press, and set aside. (2) With right sides facing, lay the side front panel to the center front. Using a ½in (1.2cm) seam allowance, machine from the waistline to the drill hole; backstitch to reinforce. Again, using a ½in (1.2cm) seam allowance, sew from the top of the pleat to the hem. Complete the other side. (3) Press the seam allowances open and press the pleats into position. (4) Turn the garment to RS and topstitch the pleats. (5) Sew the back darts and press pleat excess toward the side seams. (6) With ⅝in (1.5cm) seam allowance, machine the center back seam from the bottom of the zipper opening to the drill hole. Sew from the top of the pleat to the hem with a ½in (1.2cm) seam allowance.

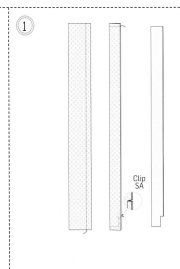

Clip SA

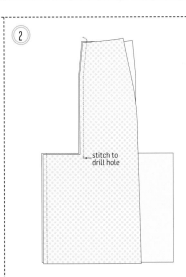

stitch to drill hole

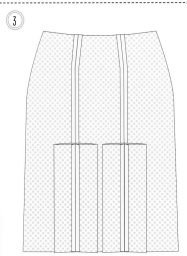

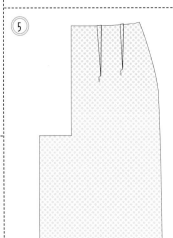

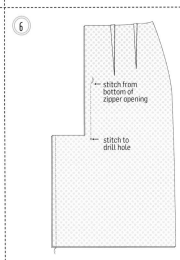

stitch from bottom of zipper opening

stitch to drill hole

▶ PATTERN TIP

This garment will translate through a range of eras: lengthen it to achieve a 1930s look or shorten it for 1960s styling.

(7) Press the seam allowances open and the pleats into position. Attach the zipper using the concealed zipper method described on page 176. Topstitch the pleats. **(8)** Place right sides together and, with a ½in (1.2cm) seam allowance, machine the side seams. **(9)** Turn the garment to RS and lay the waistband to the waist edge with right sides facing. Sew the nonmachine-basted edge of the waistband to the skirt only. **(10)** Fold the waistband into position and press the seam allowances upward into the waistband. Using the machine-basting line as a guide, fold the unsecured edge of the waistband to cover the seam allowance and edge- or sink-stitch the waistband into position. Sew a button to the underlap of the waistband and complete the buttonhole. Hem to finish.

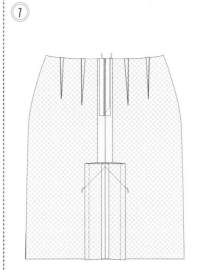

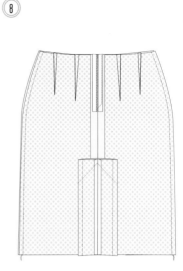

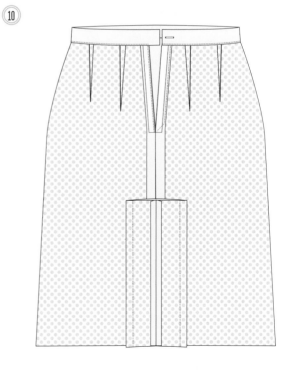

Circle skirt: 1950s

DRAFTING INSTRUCTIONS

To construct a fabric circle, you first need to know the radius of the waist opening. Use this calculation: radius = circumference ÷ 6.28.

The waistline measurement gives you the required inner circumference for your circle skirt, although it is usually best to reduce the waist measurement by 2 inches (5cm) to allow for the natural stretch as the fabric relaxes on the bias grain.

The patterns below show how to draft semicircle and circle skirts. The first step is to calculate the radius. For a semicircle skirt the radius = a to b ÷ 2; for a circle skirt the radius = a to b. Next, square off from point a, draw a quarter-circle to connect both points b, then draw another quarter-circle from c to c. The desired skirt length = b to c.

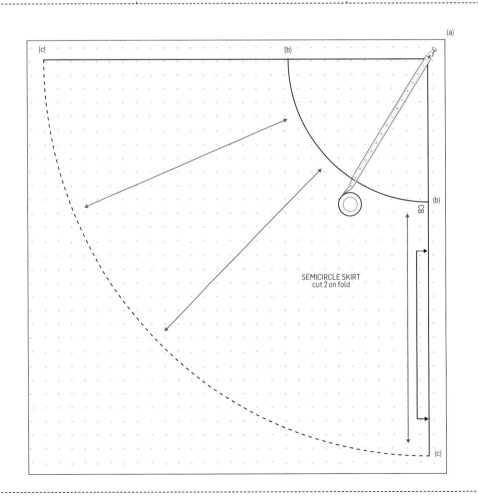

(a)

(c) (b)

(b)

CB

SEMICIRCLE SKIRT
cut 2 on fold

(c)

For a full circle, divide the waist measurement minus 2 inches (5cm) by two. Use one half as the base for making a circular section. Make a duplicate pattern from that and adjust front length.

For a circle and a half, divide the waist measurement minus 2 inches (5cm) by three. Use two-thirds for the waistline of a complete circle and the remaining one-third for the extra half-circle.

 PATTERN TIP

Varying the grain direction on circular pieces can give very different results, depending on what fabric you use. Experiment with different options.

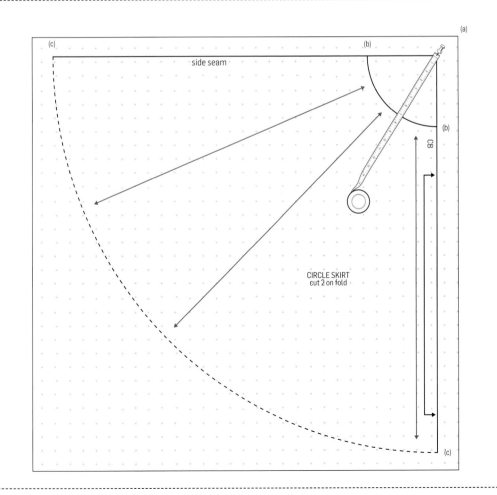

(a)

(c)   (b)

side seam

(b)

CB

CIRCLE SKIRT
cut 2 on fold

(c)

PATTERN INSTRUCTIONS

(1) Draft your circular pattern and add ½in (1.2cm) seam allowance to the side seams and waistline. Note that you will not need a seam allowance on the center front edge if you create a two-panel skirt by cutting on the fold, but you will need to add a turning allowance at the hem. The depth of this allowance depends on your desired finish: a bound seam requires only ⅜in (1cm), whereas a turned hem needs up to 1in (2.5cm). **(2)** Draft the waistband. Make a rectangle to the exact waist measurement and double the width of the finished waistband, usually between 1 and 3¼in (2.5 and 8cm). Mark the CB, CF, and side seams with notches, and the fold line with a dashed line. Add an underwrap of 1½in (4cm) and mark the buttonhole position. Cut the fabric using this pattern piece as a template, adding fusing if necessary. **(3)** With right sides together, sew the side seams and press the seam allowances open. Repeat for other panels if necessary. **(4)** Sew the CF seam. Sew the CB seam up to the bottom of the zipper opening, set the machine to its longest stitch, and machine-baste to waistline. **(5)** Press the seam allowances open and insert the zipper. Turn the garment to the right side and attach the waistband (see page 69.) You can also finish the waistband with binding or a bound-edge facing. You still need to finish the hem. Let the skirt hang overnight before finishing. This allows the fabric to relax and may necessitate hem edge leveling after a fitting. If you have used a seam allowance of 1in (2.5cm), use a gathering stitch ¼in (6mm) from the raw edge and ease to reduce the hem measurement to match the skirt.

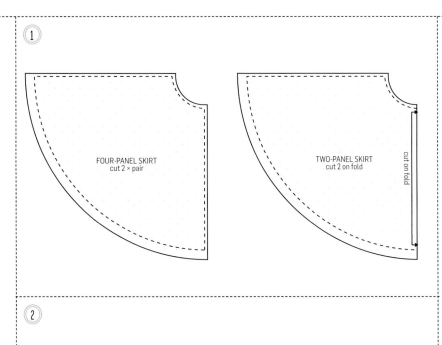

FOUR-PANEL SKIRT
cut 2 × pair

TWO-PANEL SKIRT
cut 2 on fold

cut on fold

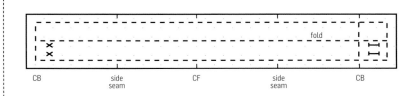

CB   side seam   CF   side seam   CB   fold

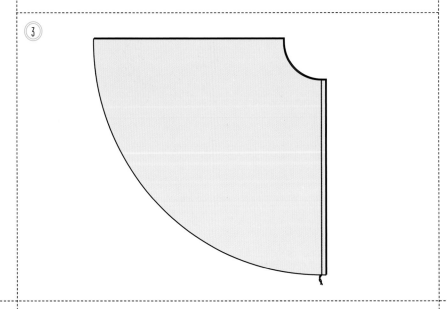

(4)

Baste zipper opening

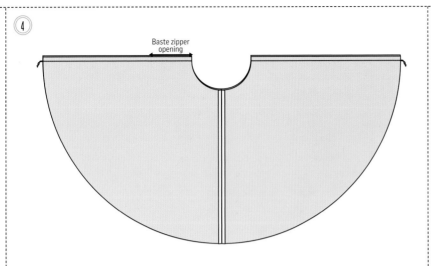

(5)

POODLE SKIRTS

Bold, solid-colored circle skirts, often featuring an appliqué motif, became a symbol of 1950s youth. These were commonly called poodle skirts, after a popular motif of the era. Included here are three appliqué motifs that can be added to your skirt. The motifs can be applied with a straight machine stitch or an edgestitch such as blanket stitch.

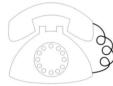

CHAPTER 4
Pants and shorts

In the early decades of the twentieth century, it was almost unthinkable for respectable women to be seen in pants, although working-class women occasionally wore men's pants for heavy laboring. Pants gradually became more common for women from the 1930s, particularly when wealthy women of leisure wore glamorous tailored pants for sporting activities or beachwear. Women began wearing more casual-looking shorts and pants for sports and leisure activities such as gardening from the 1940s onward, but skirts and dresses dominated women's wardrobes until the 1970s. That decade saw women embracing a range of denim styles from flared jeans to hotpants, while long, slim trousers for eveningwear were an elegant option. Pants and shorts are now the cornerstone of many women's wardrobes, with jeans a staple of casual wear and pant suits a core look for many working women.

Floral print playsuit.
Warehouse

Sports and leisurewear: 1930s on

THEN

At the end of the 1920s, Chanel was the first designer to show sportswear in a contemporary setting. Throughout the 1930s, beauty became inextricably linked with health. Naturist, sports, and health clubs were set up to improve both body and soul.

In Britain, the Woman's League of Health and Beauty, founded in 1930 by Prunella Stack, organized mass exercise classes in large public spaces, and similar organizations existed in other countries. Shorts started to become acceptable wear for sporty women, and ankle socks were sometimes worn instead of stockings. High waistbands were seen on the tennis court, and box-pleat shorts became popular. The late 1930s and early 1940s saw cycling outfits that included tailored knee-length culottes.

Early in the twentieth century, it was not considered important for women to win at competitive sports and so clothes were not designed to give the movement that would allow them to excel. Today, sportswear has been adapted to meet the needs of active women, and stretchy fabrics and garments such as leggings, shorts, and yoga pants have all become popular with women when exercising.

WHO: Health and good living came to the forefront for many people at this time. New fashion designs were needed to accommodate new activities.

WHY: Women were looking for items of clothing that would grant them ease of movement. Pants and shorts began to enter the mainstream.

VARIATIONS: Slacks and shorts sometimes had cuffs and center creases. Short skirts were seen on the tennis court, while culottes were worn for cycling.

SIMILAR STYLES: Wide-legged pants (shortened), page 82; French knickers, page 118

PATTERNS TO MATCH WITH: Prom dress skirt (shortened), page 26

NOW

Textured bodycon dress. *Primark Netherlands*

NOW

Aztec print trousers. *New Look*

Style and uses, then and now

FABRIC

Then: Tweed garments were often worn for golf. In the 1930s, spandex yarn began to be used in areas where stretch was needed. Breathable fibers such as cotton were also a practical choice.

Now: Rayon, viscose, and cotton are still used for shorts, while the addition of Lycra makes leggings a popular choice for workout activities. Neoprene has also risen in prominence after several designers featured the fabric on the runway.

STYLE

Then: Only worn by women who partook in sports, shorts and pants could sometimes be seen as controversial.

Now: Tailored shorts are more than acceptable for both day and evening casual wear, with creases and belts often included in the design.

COLORS

Then: In 1932, American tennis champion Alice Marble caused a sensation by wearing white shorts on the tennis court. Green, navy, and tweed were other popular colors for sportswear.

Now: A variety of colors are worn today and the limits are seemingly endless. Bright and neon tones are often used, while white is still a traditional look for tennis, and is the stipulated color for competitors at Wimbledon.

MATCHED WITH:

Then: Shorts and pants often came as part of a suit that included a bolero-style jacket teamed with a wide leather belt. Low, thick heels were worn on the feet and cotton tops were worn for tennis.

Now: Crop tops and sports bras are used when in the gym and sport-specific sneakers may be worn. Shorts are often teamed with blouson tops for an air of dressed-down elegance.

NOW

Drawstring shorts. *Fat Face*

NOW

Leisure pants. *River Island*

SEWING TIPS

- To prevent snags or runs on jersey fabrics, use ballpoint needles. These have a blunt end, which will sew between the threads of a knitted fabric.

- Sew stretch fabric with a shallow machine zigzag stitch. This will add some give to seams and prevent them snapping during wear.

- Use a stretch fusing to provide support for facings or collars and a cotton tape or bias fusing tape to prevent stretch at problem areas such as shoulders or necklines.

The playsuit: 1930s / 1970s

In the late 1920s and early 1930s, beach pajamas started becoming popular as a cover-up over swimsuits, often as a two-piece set of jacket and pants. By the mid-1930s, the popular type of beach pajama was a one-piece jumpsuit style with a wide leg, often made of crêpe de chine or silk.

A variation on these, often worn for sports, was the playsuit. This was an all-in-one shorts and shirt combination that often came with a detachable skirt to be worn over the shorts in public.

In the 1970s, the beach pajama was reincarnated as the jumpsuit. Made in elegant draping fabrics such as satin or jersey, it made glamorous eveningwear. These days, modern jumpsuits and playsuits are often made in stretch fabrics such as jersey or Lycra. They rarely come with a detachable skirt and are considered acceptable attire for day or evening.

THEN

WHO: Coco Chanel designed beach pajamas as part of the Riviera look.

WHY: A glamorous yet practical style.

VARIATIONS: Dungarees or overalls

SIMILAR STYLES: Sports and leisurewear, page 76

PATTERNS TO MATCH WITH: 1920s slip, page 114; French knickers, page 118

NOW

Jumpsuit shorts. *Sugar Hill Boutique*

NOW

Trackstar Limited playsuit. *Marks & Spencer*

Style and uses, then and now

FABRIC

Then: Made in silk or new synthetics like crêpe de chine, or occasionally toweling for beachwear. Playsuits were often made from cotton or rayon.

Now: Stretch fabrics like jersey, or fabrics with added Lycra, are popular for ease of movement and comfort.

LENGTH

Then: Beach pajamas were normally full-length pants, while shorter playsuits often came with an attached knee-length skirt for modesty.

Now: Playsuits can be very short.

STYLE

Then: Beach pajamas and playsuits often came in two-piece sets featuring pants or jumpsuit and a matching jacket, or a playsuit with a matching skirt. They were worn for sports or leisurewear only.

Now: Jumpsuits in draping fabrics are often worn as an alternative to an evening dress, while shorter playsuits are popular for summer daywear.

COLORS

Then: The popular Art Deco style of the 1930s meant that geometric patterns and bright colors were common. Chinese and Japanese designs were also used and considered very exotic.

Now: Black is a popular color as it is considered flattering with such a body-skimming style. For day, floral prints are most commonly seen, but the more daring might use bright colors or metallics to make a statement for eveningwear.

MATCHED WITH

Then: As both styles were designed as leisure- or sportswear, they were worn over swimsuits and teamed most often with flat or low-heeled shoes or sandals suitable for the beach or for active pursuits.

Now: A jumpsuit might be worn extra-long, covering high heels to create an elegant, elongated silhouette for evening. Playsuits can be worn with flats for a more casual style by day or with heels for a more glamorous evening look.

NOW

SEWING TIPS

• Use a drawstring or elasticated waist to give a relaxed feel to a jumpsuit. If the style does not have a seam at the waistline for elastic or cord insertion, use a bias strip of fabric to create a channel. This can be used on the inside or outside of your garment.

• If using a corded waist finish on the inside of your garment, create buttonhole openings to allow for the cord to be threaded and tied on the right side.

Kiku jumpsuit. *Phase Eight*

Denim: 1950s on

THEN

Denim, and denim jeans in particular, has a long history. Where and how exactly the trend began is still being debated, but denim is indisputably a part of everyday fashion life and has been so for decades.

The majority of sources suggest that the word "denim" derives from the English translation of the French city of Nîmes and the sturdy serge fabric produced there. Originally called "serge de Nîmes," this eventually transmuted into "denim." This was a hardwearing, sturdy fabric ideal for producing garments suitable for heavy laboring.

The Levi Strauss company is credited with inventing denim jeans, and by the 1950s many laborers preferred wearing Levi jeans to overalls for work. Brands such as Lee Cooper and Wrangler also became famous, with each brand known for its own particular cut. Teenagers started to adopt jeans as a fashion item in the 1950s. By the late 1960s and early 1970s, blue jeans had become a universal uniform for teenagers and young adults. Today, jeans are still a staple part of both women's and men's wardrobes, and people of all ages wear them.

WHO: By the 1970s, jeans were a staple garment for almost every teenager and young adult.

WHY: The mass manufacturing of styles occurred at this time and desirable designer labels became more sought-after.

VARIATIONS: Daisy Duke shorts, denim jackets, denim skirts, and a variety of jean cuts were all made and worn.

SIMILAR STYLES: Wide-legged pants, page 82

PATTERNS TO MATCH WITH: Blouse, page 54; 1920s slip (camisole version), page 114; 1940s slip (camisole version), page 120

NOW

Distressed denim. *Warehouse*

NOW

Traditional indigo blue denim. *Apricot*

Style and uses, then and now

FABRICS

Then: Denim was made of sturdy cotton twill woven from white and blue threads. The 1970s introduced the pre-washed effect, which led to the growth of different denim styles.

Now: The same basic techniques for weaving denim still exist, although there are now many different ways to treat the denim to achieve a variety of looks. Lycra may be added to offer stretch to the denim. Organic denim is increasingly available due to the rise in production of organic cotton.

LENGTH

Then: Jean lengths in the 1970s were often long, in keeping with that decade's typically elongated silhouette. Styles were often so long that they touched the floor.

Now: Available in every length, at present cropped designs are growing in popularity, along with styles that can be turned up.

STYLE

Then: Worn by young people to rock music concerts and for everyday life, denim and jeans became the uniform for "cool."

Now: Worn by all ages, jeans are the go-to style for casual daywear. They can be dressed up for evening, and the variety in cuts means they are appropriate for various occasions.

COLORS

Then: Indigo blue denim was the color that most people wore, with lighter blues popular in the flared styles of the 1970s.

Now: Denim now is still traditionally blue, though recent trends have seen women wearing bright, vibrant tones as well as black and gray versions.

MATCHED WITH

Then: Worn with long jackets, band T-shirts, midriff-bearing tops, and platform shoes, denim was ideally suited to the carefree nature of the 1970s.

Now: Worn with boots, sandals, high heels, fitted tops, leather jackets, and blouses, jeans have become such a versatile choice for both day and night that they can be partnered with almost anything.

SEWING TIPS

- Use a heavyweight topstitch thread in a contrasting color to make decorative stitching stand out.

- Use a jeans machine needle to reduce skipped stitches.

- To distress denim and give your item a lived-in vintage feel, use sandpaper.

NOW

Bootleg jeans. *MiH*

Wide-legged pants: 1930s / 1960s / 1970s

GARMENT SPECS

These wide-legged pants echo both 1930s leisurewear and the flared styles of the 1960s and 1970s, depending on fabric choice. Suitable for a variety of fabrics.

STYLE VARIATIONS

You can add a straight waistband for this style. Simply measure the waist and create a rectangle using this measurement plus double the desired height. You could also add a patch pocket (see page 174).

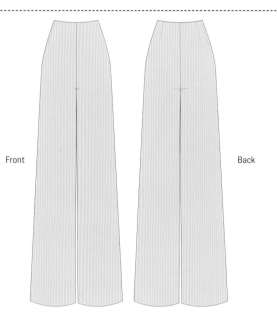

Front

Back

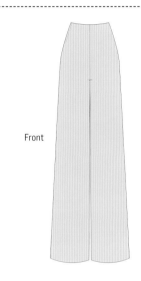

Front

Back

Sizes	S (in)	S (cm)	M (in)	M (cm)	L (in)	L (cm)	XL (in)	XL (cm)
Waist on top seam	25¼	64.2	27¼	69.2	29³⁄₁₆	74.2	31³⁄₁₆	79.2
Waistband width	1⁹⁄₁₆	4	1⁹⁄₁₆	4	1⁹⁄₁₆	4	1⁹⁄₁₆	4
Hip 3¹⁵⁄₁₆in (10cm) below waistband at side seam	33¹⁄₁₆	84	35¹⁄₁₆	89	37	94	39	99
Hip 8⅝in (22cm) below waistband at side seam	38¹⁄₁₆	96.6	40	101.6	41⁵⁄₁₆	106.6	43¹⁵⁄₁₆	111.6
Thigh	26⅛	66.4	27⅛	68.9	28⅛	71.4	29⅛	73.9
Hem	27⅛	68.9	27¾	70.5	28⅜	72.1	29	73.7
Inside leg	29¹³⁄₁₆	75.7	29¹³⁄₁₆	75.7	29¹³⁄₁₆	75.7	29¹³⁄₁₆	75.7
Outside leg including waistband	42⅝	108.2	42⅞	108.9	43⅛	109.6	43⁷⁄₁₆	110.3
Front rise	11¾	29.9	12¹⁄₁₆	30.7	12⅜	31.5	12¹¹⁄₁₆	32.3
Back rise	14⁵⁄₁₆	36.3	14⅝	37.1	14⅞	37.9	15¼	38.7

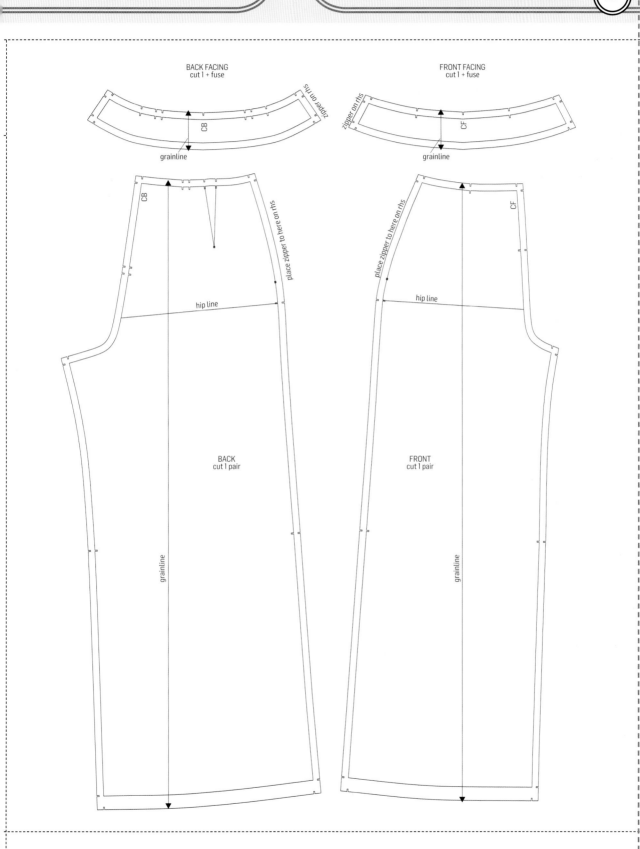

BACK FACING
cut 1 + fuse

FRONT FACING
cut 1 + fuse

CB

grainline

zipper on rhs

CF

grainline

zipper on rhs

CB

place zipper to here on rhs

zipper on rhs

hip line

BACK
cut 1 pair

grainline

CF

place zipper to here on rhs

hip line

FRONT
cut 1 pair

grainline

PATTERN INSTRUCTIONS

(1) Prepare the facing. With right sides together, sew the left-hand side of the facing, leaving the right-hand side open for the zipper. Neaten the lower edge with a ½in (12mm) single turn and set aside. (2) Sew the darts on the back waists and press toward the side seam. (3) With right sides facing, sew the front and back together at the LHS seam. On the RHS, set the machine to its longest stitch and sew from the waist to the zipper insertion point. Return the machine stitch to its usual stitch length, make a couple of backstitches to reinforce the opening, and sew to the hem. Press the seam allowances open. (4) With RS together, sew the inside leg seams and press the seam allowances open. (5) Turn one leg to the right side and insert into the other leg. Ensuring right sides are together, sew CF rise seam in one. (6) Insert the zipper on the RHS using the concealed zipper method (see page 176). Turn the pants to the right side and unpick the basting stitches to release opening. With RS together, lay the facing on the waist and sew into position. Understitch through the facing and seam allowances only. (7) Press the facing into position and fold and finish the facing with a handstitch at the zipper (see page 29 for more detail on this). Hem to finish.

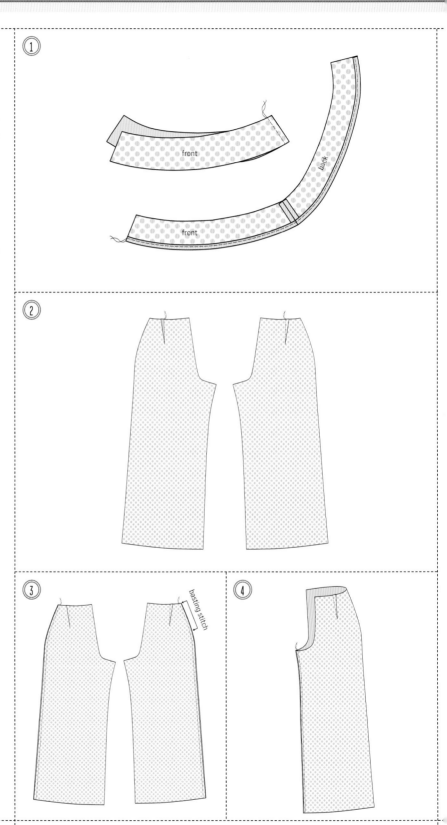

⑤

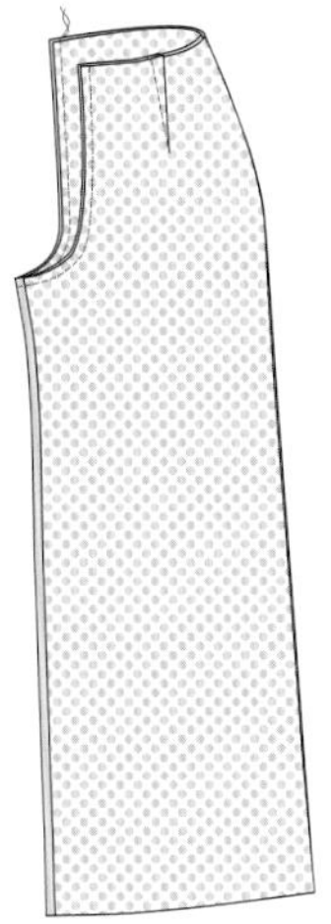

⑥

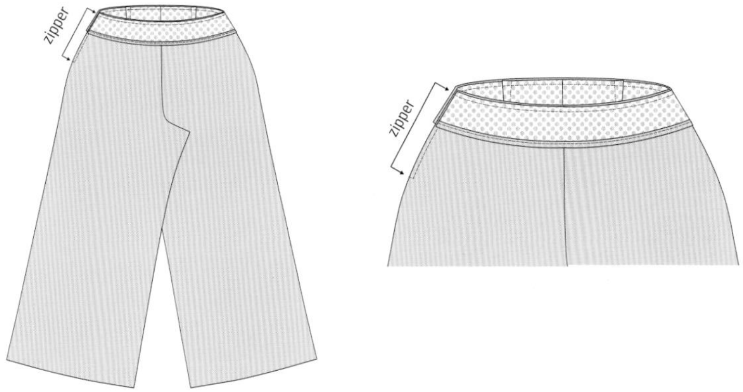

zipper

zipper

⑦

zipper

zipper

CHAPTER 5

Suits and coats

Women's suits of the 1920s through the 1940s consisted of a jacket and a matching skirt. These garments tended to be plain and functional rather than chic, made in hardwearing and long-lasting fabrics such as serge and tweed. Yves Saint Laurent first made the pant suit an elegant option for women's eveningwear in the 1960s with his "Le Smoking" tuxedo suit, and since then pant suits as well as the traditional skirt suit have been adopted by many professional women. Coats for women have often been influenced by menswear, from the parka beloved by the mods of the 1960s, through to the perennially popular leather biker jacket, and military-inspired heavyweight woolen coats that are a smart option for cold weather.

Yellow coat. *Orla Kiely*

The utility coat: 1940s / 1950s

THEN

In line with the austerity measures brought in during World War II, Boards of Trade in the U.K. and the U.S.A. introduced restrictions on the use of raw materials and labor that affected clothing production. In Britain, clothing was rationed, and austerity-approved designs were brought in that used fabric in the least wasteful way.

Top designers of the time such as Edward Molyneux, Digby Morton, Hardy Amies, and Peter Russell were commissioned to design a year-round wardrobe comprising an overcoat, suit (with shirt or blouse), and day dress. Templates in graded sizes were made of 32 of these designs and they became available to manufacturers for a small fee in October 1942. From that point, style restrictions were turned from a negative to a positive, with the focus on cut and line. Styles became simple and pared-down.

Military-style detailing was incorporated into the designs, and belts, breast pockets, high necks, and small collars all featured on utility-style coats. These accouterments are still popular today, and military-style coats with features such as a square-shouldered silhouette, epaulettes, and embossed metal buttons are classic fashion items.

WHO: Various trading laws were passed during wartime to prevent fabric wastage. Designers created simple capsule collections for manufacturers to replicate.

WHY: Utility coats were simple, with button detailing and self-tie belts, and had a military flavor. Wasteful cutting was forbidden, and a list of constraints was introduced such as minimal trimmings and restrictions on the number of buttons and pockets a garment could have.

VARIATIONS: Single-breasted and double-breasted overcoats kept variations to the minimum. Removable belts offered a point of difference at the waist.

SIMILAR STYLES: Fitted jacket, p. 96; box jacket, p. 102

PATTERNS TO MATCH WITH: Box-pleated skirt, page 66; wide-legged pants, page 82

NOW

Kala coat. *Monsoon*

NOW

A modern-day take on the utility look. *Elégance*

Style and uses, then and now

FABRIC

Then: Hardwearing and understated, wool was commonly used to make utility coats.

Now: Military-style coats are still often made from wool, with synthetic fabrics such as viscose and polyester making up cheaper options. Cashmere may be added to more expensive designs.

LENGTH

Then: Styles that fell just below the knee were seen as fashionable, demure, and functional. This was in keeping with the most common skirt length of the period.

Now: Utility overcoat styles still often fall just below the knee, although a variety of lengths may be seen. Some coats fall only to the hip.

STYLE

Then: Long coats often had collars with revers and fell straight to the ground with very minimal pleat detailing, due to the restrictions. Additional surface interest was created by the imaginative design and placement of buttons.

Now: Styles are often double-breasted. Buckled belts and epaulettes on the shoulders add to the military effect, while hoods may be added to give a design a modern edge.

COLORS

Then: A somber palette was used during wartime: sage green, navy blue, and light brown. This very much mirrored the uniforms of the armed forces.

Now: The design house Balmain has become known for its utility styles, with green, navy, and red prominent colors. Designs often have clashing buttons and chains, with sequin embellishments added for effect.

MATCHED WITH

Then: Paired with simple day dresses, nylon stockings, clip-on earrings, and leather laced shoes, the overcoat was long-lasting and much needed in the cold winter months.

Now: Skinny jeans and pin-thin heeled boots often partner military coats. This slim, elongated look balances out the heavy nature of the coat, flattering the silhouette.

SEWING TIPS

- Check fabrics for shrinkage before cutting out and sewing; fabrics with a high wool content are liable to shrink during construction when steam is applied and during laundering.

- Highlight design elements such as openings, collars, and pockets with topstitching.

- Use good-quality tailoring fusing for facings, collar, and pockets to avoid fabric becoming overly rigid; this will spoil the appearance of the finished garment.

A crisp silhouette and strong shoulders give a modern military look. (Model's own)

The utility jacket: 1940s / 1950s

THEN

Wartime America brought in the L85 restriction scheme on clothing, which banned design elements that used extraneous fabric, such as double yokes, sashes, turn-up cuffs, and patch pockets. With these regulations in place, along with restrictions on the use of raw materials and labor, fashion was forced to become simple and functional, much like the utility clothing that was introduced in Britain.

The 1941 British Board of Trade restrictions ensured that low- to medium-quality consumer goods were produced to the highest possible standards at reasonable prices, consistent with the restrictions on raw material and labor. To further economize on diminishing resources, the Making of Civilian Clothing (Restriction Orders) was passed in 1942. This forbade wasteful cutting and set out a list of restraints within which dressmakers, tailors, and manufacturers were compelled to work.

Despite the restrictions, some wartime clothing still managed to be stylish. Women served in both British and U.S. auxiliary forces, and those in the U.S. were considered to have the most glamorous uniforms, many of which had been designed by top fashion talents. Mainbocher was especially praised for blending functionality with femininity.

So-called Eisenhower jackets, a military-influenced design, became popular during this period. This style was bloused at the chest and fitted at the waist with a belt. Often reconstructed from traditional men's styles, these jackets had a boxy effect. This feature is often still present in today's utility- and military-inspired designs, with nipped-in waists hinting at the 1950s silhouette.

WHO: Women serving in auxiliary forces and everyone adhering to wartime utility restrictions on clothing designs.

WHY: Jacket designs had to be simple and pared-down due to the wartime restrictions put in place to keep material wastage and labor time down.

VARIATIONS: Styles were short and boxy or long and lean, with pronounced shoulders and nipped-in waists.

SIMILAR STYLES: Fitted jacket, page 96; box jacket, page 102

PATTERNS TO MATCH WITH: Blouse, page 54; box-pleated skirt, page 64; wide-legged pants, page 82

NOW

Jacket with utility detailing. *Oxfam Fashion*

Style and uses, then and now

FABRIC

Then: With materials restrictions in place, the fabrics used were simple; often cotton and wool.

Now: Synthetic fibers are now more popular than ever, with polyester present in many designs.

LENGTH

Then: The silhouette was narrow and tailored with pronounced shoulders and a narrow waist. The alternative to the long and narrow look was a short and boxy jacket.

Now: Jackets today usually fall to the hip, although the cropped style has been revived in recent years.

STYLE

Then: Worn by women who were often recruited to take over the jobs of men who were away fighting, jackets were seen as functional, smart, and professional. Buttons added some interest where the jacket style was generally extremely simple.

Now: Military styles are often double-breasted with the emphasis still on the buttons. Lapels are bigger than they were and patch pockets have returned.

COLORS

Then: A somber palette was generally used to match the mood of the era. Sage green, navy blue, and light brown tones were common, although more vibrant colors were reintroduced at the start of the 1950s.

Now: With wartime restrictions long over, utility-style jackets come in varied colors. Button detailing still offers wearers a point of interest, and although the cut remains simple, sequins, vibrant tones, and metallic hues are now all popular.

MATCHED WITH

Then: Matched with skirts of the same fabric, the look was smart and professional rather than feminine. Ladies often wore utility jackets with pencil skirts, simple blouses, low-heeled shoes, and day dresses.

Now: The utility-style jacket is now often used to smarten up a casual look, and is commonly partnered with jeans. The cut is still boxy, while nipped-in waist styles give a more tailored effect.

SEWING TIPS

- Lay out fabric pieces to asses the positioning of a patterned fabric: matching a stripe or plaid requires more care and fabric than matching a plain fabric.

- Cut patterned fabric singly rather than on the fold or in pairs.

- If you require symmetry, trace the dominant elements of a pattern onto the paper pattern to ensure accurate matching.

- Cut pockets on a bias grain and interface to prevent stretching.

NOW

Utility style jacket with rever collar. *ASOS*

The utility skirt: 1940s / 1950s

THEN

During World War II, both the U.S.A. and the U.K. brought in austerity measures including restrictions on the use of raw materials to prevent wastage of scarce resources. Under the measures that affected clothing, one of the stipulations was that skirts (among other garments) should be simple in design with almost no excessive detailing and unnecessary use of fabric.

In the U.S., Regulation L85 was passed in 1942, specifying restrictions on all sorts of clothing. In the case of skirts, full-skirted garments such as dirndl skirts were forbidden, so utility-approved skirts were slim and unfussy in silhouette. Throughout war-torn Europe and America, it was acceptable for women to wear pants for utilitarian purposes, in the country, on the beach, or in the form of dressy evening slacks. For other occasions, the rule of thumb was: if in doubt, wear a skirt.

The pared-down and minimalist utility skirt gradually evolved into the more glamorous pencil skirt; this is still a popular and smart look for women, encouraging them to show off their figure and walk with a wiggle.

WHO: Designers of the time were commissioned to design simple, pared-down styles that could be easily replicated.

WHY: Restrictions on materials and labor meant war-time skirt designs had to be unfussy, with the focus on cut and line.

VARIATIONS: Skirts were straight, had kick or inverted pleats, or had gently flared panels to facilitate movement.

SIMILAR STYLES: Fitted jacket, page 96; box jacket, page 102

PATTERNS TO MATCH WITH: Blouse, page 54; box-pleated skirt, page 66; wide-legged pants, page 82

NOW

Trapeze skirt. *Hobbs*

NOW

Modern elegance in a utility-style skirt. *Dreamstime*

Style and uses, then and now

FABRIC

Then: American-produced crisp cotton was used in abundance by designers and manufacturers, many of whom had previously imported French fabrics.

Now: Modern takes on the utility style are seen in a wide variety of fabrics. In recent years, leather and suede have become popular choices.

LENGTH

Then: Hemlines reached about 18 inches (46cm) from the ground—generally just at or near knee length.

Now: A popular skirt length is often just above the knee. Slimmer styles often sit at calf length.

STYLE

Then: Utility-era skirts had to be functional, hardwearing, and versatile. The lines were simple and clean.

Now: Pencil skirts and inverted pleat styles offer elegant simplicity in today's fashion scene. They can be worn in professional situations and for evening attire.

COLORS

Then: Red was a common color for utility-approved clothing, as the military commandeered brown and green dyes for uniforms.

Now: Simple utility-type styles often feature block colors with minimal detailing. Peacock blue is a popular choice.

MATCHED WITH

Then: Worn with simply constructed matching jackets with small lapels and rever collars, nylon stockings (silk was requisitioned for the war effort), chic blouses, heeled shoes, intricate hairstyles, and fully madeup faces.

Now: The utility effect on skirts means that slim styles are often paired with biker jackets and oversized blouses to offer a contrast. The skirt suit is still a popular choice for professional women, as the look is considered both smart and demure.

NOW

Bryony skirt. *Hobbs.*

NOW

Pencil skirt with high slit. *Simply Be*

SEWING TIPS

• For an easy design variation, divide a pencil pattern into a paneled skirt. Mark panel lines onto an existing pattern and trace panels to create a copy. Add a seam allowance where necessary.

• Consider varying the grain positioning on a patterned fabric.

• To give a fishtail look, add godets between panels.

The kimono jacket: 1950s

THEN

The kimono is a traditional style of Japanese dress, while the kimono-style jacket became a popular, opulent take on the look as interpreted by Western fashion designers in the 1950s.

The adoption of Eastern styles into Western high fashion is nothing new; the influence of Asian costume was seen in the work of designers such as Paul Poiret and, later, Yves Saint Laurent. The traditional Japanese kimono was worn by both men and women, although men's styles tended to be less elaborate. The kimono as worn by women could be heavy and cumbersome and usually required assistance to put on. The continuing popularity of the kimono is partly due to the very beautiful, ornate, and lavishly embroidered designs in rich materials, particularly heavy silks. Kimono designs often included motifs from nature and were worn at the appropriate season; for example, a kimono featuring cherry-blossom patterns would be worn in the spring.

Contemporary designers such as Diane von Furstenberg, L'Wren Scott, and Louis Vuitton have featured looks in their collections that have been influenced by Eastern style. The kimono-style jacket, with its voluminous sleeves, is a stylish alternative to a cardigan or a lightweight jacket.

WHO: The Japanese and those who could afford high-end Eastern-inspired fashion designs.

WHY: Designers in the West started to look further afield for their fashion inspiration.

VARIATION: Formal kimonos were worn for special occasions such as weddings; more casual styles in lighter fabrics and plainer designs were made for everyday wear.

SIMILAR STYLES: Box jacket, page 102

PATTERNS TO MATCH WITH: Wide-legged pants, page 82

NOW

NOW

Tulip kimono (www.decadesofstyle.com). *Decades of Style Pattern Company*

Traditional kimono with *obi* belt. *Takayukiworld*

Style and uses, then and now

FABRICS

Then: Made from silk, silk brocade, silk crêpe, and satin weave for everyday and eveningwear. Detailed embroidery was also a significant feature.

Now: Silk is still the most popular fabric choice, although kimonos for more casual wear are available in cotton and polyester.

LENGTH

Then: Traditional kimonos are full-length and elaborately layered garments with full, billowing sleeves.

Now: Traditional styles are still full-length, while styles seen on the runway are often shorter and easier to wear. Today, most Japanese people who wear a kimono choose the simpler style known as *yukata*. These are more casual in style, unlined, and usually made in a lightweight fabric such as cotton.

STYLE

Then: Signaling the exotic and the Oriental, the Western-style Japanese kimono was worn shorter and had more of a lightweight jacket effect.

Now: Kimonos worn for fashion nowadays have been adapted for everyday life and casualwear. Traditional Japanese styles worn with accessories such as *obi* belts are still very much a part of Japanese culture.

COLORS

Then: Kimonos for formal occasions were expensive items often made in rich-colored silks and brocades. Duck-egg blue designs with gold embroidery were a chic designer way to wear the style.

Now: Kimonos come in an array of colors, with red, purple, and white printed pattern styles the most recent decadent choice.

MATCHED WITH

Then: Worn in Japan with traditional makeup and accessories, the style can only be worn with other authentic designs. In the 1950s, when the style was seen in high-end designer collections, it was often paired with a pencil skirt.

Now: Seen in an array of colors and styles, the shorter Western-style kimono is now often paired with jeans and worn over a plain white T-shirt.

SEWING TIPS

- With any lightweight fabric, use a spray-on fabric stabilizer or sandwich fabric between pattern or tissue paper when cutting.

- Sew hems and profile edges carefully to reduce stretch.

- Make a padded *obi* belt with an interlining of felt. After turning out, give your belt an authentic quilted look by adding lines of spaced topstitching.

NOW

Fringed kimono. *Internacionale*

NOW

Tropical kimono. *Alwear*

Fitted jacket 1930s / 1940s

⏵⏵ GARMENT SPEC

This jacket has a shaped roll collar, two-part tailored sleeve, and can be constructed with or without a lining. These instructions are for an unlined jacket with a bound internal finish. (For the lining method, see box jacket on page 102). Suitable for a wide variety of medium-weight fabrics.

Sizes	S (in)	S (cm)	M (in)	M (cm)	L (in)	L (cm)	XL (in)	XL (cm)
Bust at armhole	35¼	89.6	37¼	94.6	39³⁄₁₆	99.6	41³⁄₁₆	104.6
Waist 7¹⁄₁₆in (18cm) below armhole	27	68.6	29	73.6	30¹⁵⁄₁₆	78.6	32¹⁵⁄₁₆	83.6
Hem on seam	37⁵⁄₁₆	94.8	39⁵⁄₁₆	99.8	41¼	104.8	43¼	109.8
Shoulder	4¹¹⁄₁₆	11.9	4¹³⁄₁₆	12.2	4¹⁵⁄₁₆	12.5	5¹⁄₁₆	12.8
CB length to hem	23⁷⁄₁₆	59.6	23¹¹⁄₁₆	60.2	23¹⁵⁄₁₆	60.8	24³⁄₁₆	61.4
Back neck on seam	5¼	13.4	5½	14	5¾	14.6	6	15.2
Collar depth at CB	3⅛	8	3⅛	8	3⅛	8	3⅛	8
Wrist	8⅜	21.2	8¹¹⁄₁₆	22	9	22.8	9⁵⁄₁₆	23.6
Sleeve length	22½	57.2	22¹¹⁄₁₆	57.6	22¹³⁄₁₆	58	23	58.4

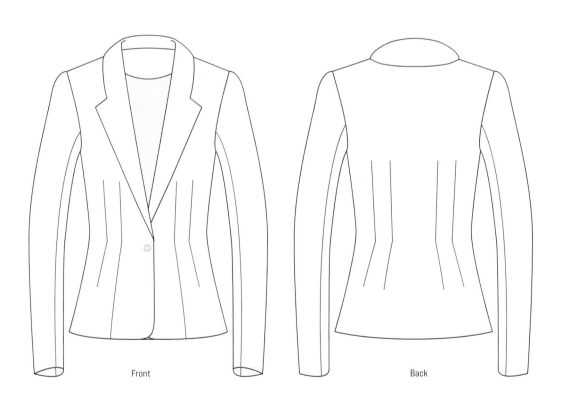

Front   Back

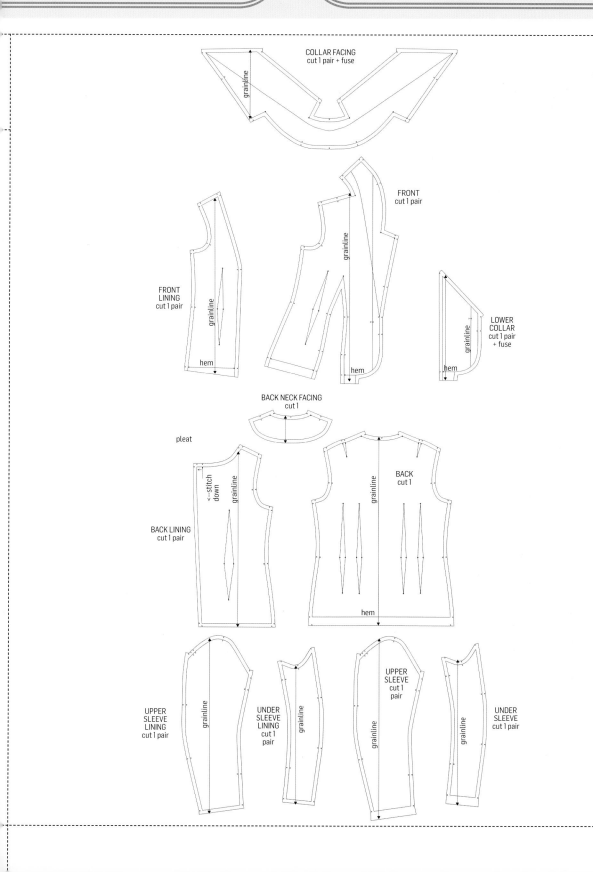

PATTERN INSTRUCTIONS

(1) Prepare the facing. With right sides together, sew the lower collar facing to the collar facing. Press the seam allowances open. (2) Join the neckline facing to the collar facing. With right sides together, sew to the drill hole; ensure that the needle is lowered through the work, and snip into collar facing section only. Pivot the work and sew back neckline to the next drill hole. Again, lower the needle through the work and snip into the collar facing corner to release fabric and pivot work. Sew to end. Miter the corner of the neck facing, understitch the seam allowances to the neckline facing, and press. (3) Bind the collar facing edge. (4) Prepare the sleeves. Set the machine to its longest stitch and sew two lines of gathering stitch as shown in the diagram. (5) Return the machine to its regular stitch length. Match the notches on the sleeve seam, noting how the sleeves are not a perfect match. Use machine basting stitch to ease the under-sleeve to the upper sleeve. Bind the seam. (6) Bind the sleeve hem. (7) Sew the other sleeve seam and bind. Fold and neaten the hem edge of the binding to ensure a raw binding edge does not show. (8) Match the notches and sew the large front dart. Bind the dart, neatening the upper edge of the binding. Sew the rest of the darts on the front and back sections using the usual method.

PATTERN TIP

Ensure that all drill holes are marked with a tailor's tack or alternative marking technique to facilitate matching of precise points during construction.

①

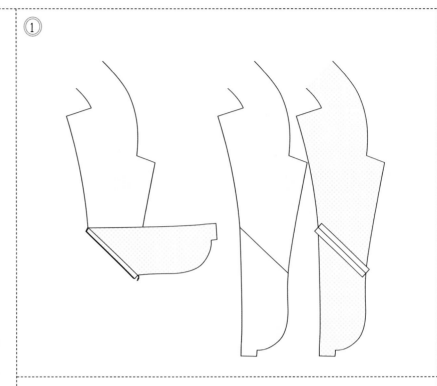

②

snip collar facing corner
only and pivot work

miter neck facing

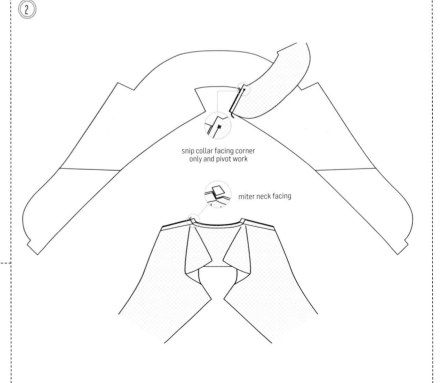

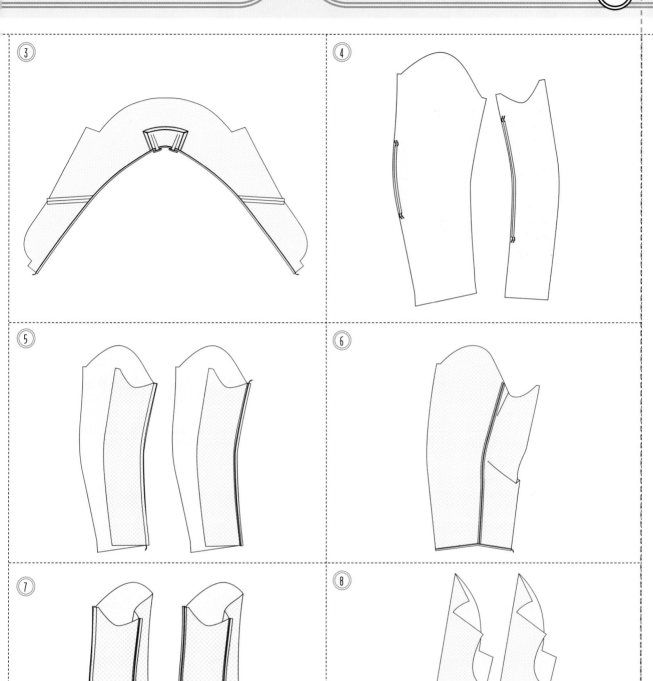

(9) Bind the front and back side seams.
(10) Sew front panels together at center
back neck seam. (11) Sew the front and back
neckline, following the procedure described
in step 2. When you reach the drill hole, snip
the front section only, allowing the work to
be pivoted. (12) After the seam is completed,
miter the back section as shown in step 2.
Bind the shoulder seams; it is not practical
to bind right to the end of the neck edge of
the shoulder seam, as this is both fiddly and
bulky. As this portion of the shoulder will be
hidden by the collar facing, sew only as far
as shown. (13) With right sides together, sew
the collar facing and main jacket together
along the profile edge. Turn to right side and
press, using a cardboard pressing template
if required. This profile edge can be
topstitched after construction if desired.
(14) Sew the side seams and press the seam
allowances open. Press the shoulder seam
binding toward the back. (15) Insert the sleeve
using the method described on page 162.
Bind the armhole, encasing all layers.
You will need to neaten the binding finishing
to prevent any raw edges being on show.
Bind the hem all in one, fold up the hem,
and blindstitch it into position. Fold the sleeve
hem and blindstitch it in place. Make the
buttonhole and sew on the button.

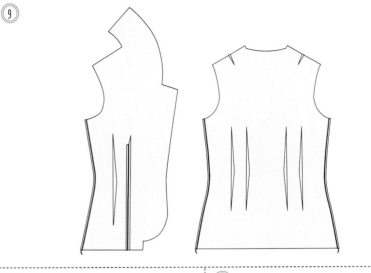

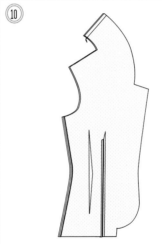

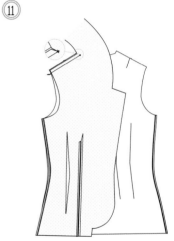

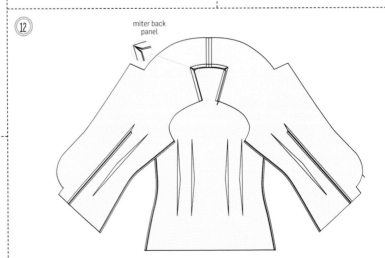

miter back
panel

 PATTERN TIP

Don't fold and neaten the ends of binding
sections unless the instructions say to, as
this will cause unnecessary bulk.

⑬

⑭

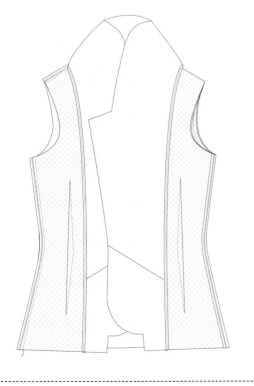

⑮

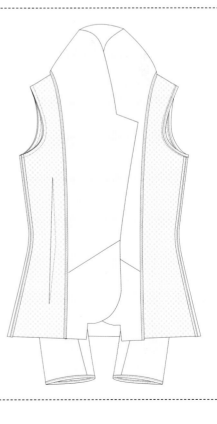

Box jacket: 1960s

GARMENT SPEC

This lined box-pleated jacket has raglan sleeves. It can be worn in combination with a knee-length A-line skirt to make a 1960s-style skirt suit. This design is suitable for medium- to heavyweight fabrics such as wool or bouclé. Finish with a contrast braid.

Sizes	S (in)	S (cm)	M (in)	M (cm)	L (in)	L (cm)	XL (in)	XL (cm)
Bust at armhole	35 11/16	90.6	37 5/8	95.6	39 5/8	100.6	41 9/16	105.6
Hem on seam	32 5/16	82	34 1/4	87	36 1/4	92	38 3/16	97
CB length to hem	16 5/8	42.2	16 7/8	42.8	17 1/16	43.4	17 5/16	44
Back neck on seam	6 7/16	16.4	6 11/16	17	6 15/16	17.6	7 3/16	18.2
Cuff	10 1/16	25.5	10 3/8	26.3	10 11/16	27.1	11	27.9
Sleeve length from the neck	27 1/2	69.9	27 13/16	70.7	28 1/8	71.5	28 7/16	72.3

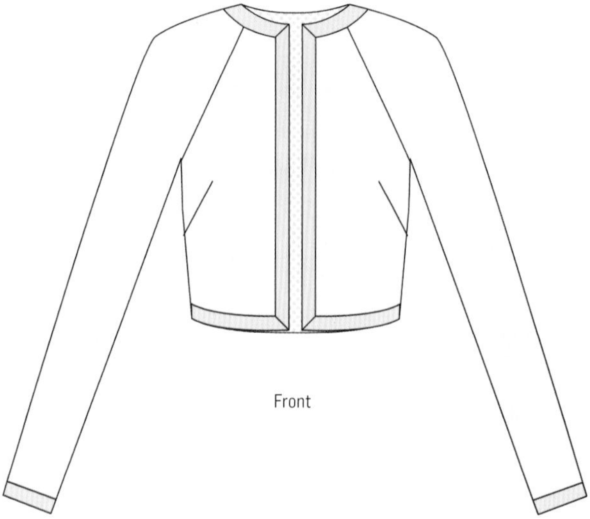
Front

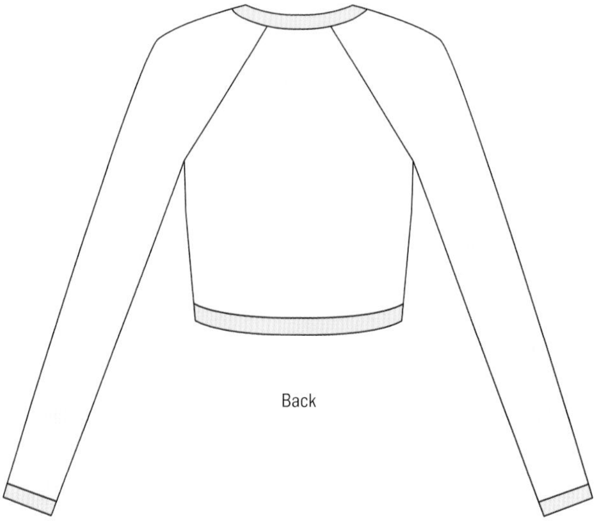
Back

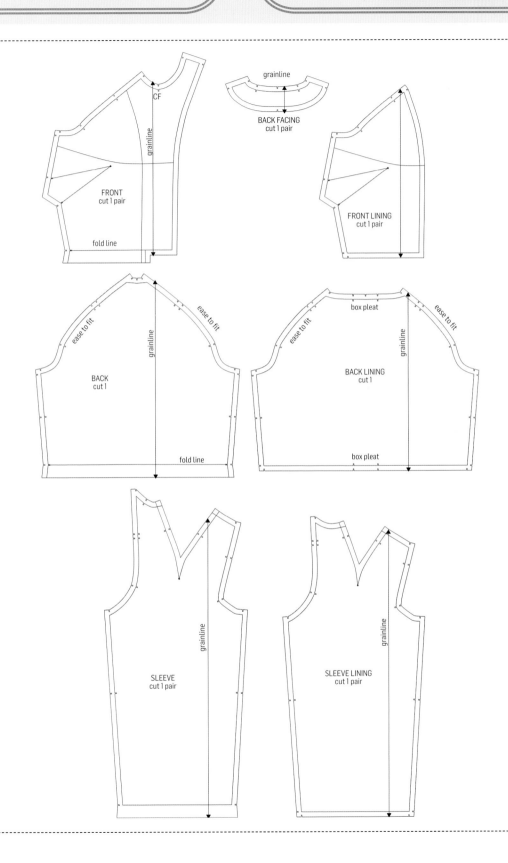

FRONT
cut 1 pair

BACK FACING
cut 1 pair

FRONT LINING
cut 1 pair

BACK
cut 1

BACK LINING
cut 1

SLEEVE
cut 1 pair

SLEEVE LINING
cut 1 pair

PATTERN INSTRUCTIONS

(1) With right sides together, fold the sleeve and sew shoulder darts on both raglan sleeves. (2) Press the seam allowances open at the shoulder. (3) Sew the darts on the front pieces and press the dart excess toward the hem. (4) With right sides facing, join the front of the raglan sleeve to the jacket front. Repeat for the other side.
(5) Place right sides together and join the back sleeve to the jacket back. Repeat for other side. The jacket is now joined at all four sleeve seams. (6) Next, press the sleeve seam allowances open, snipping seam allowances to release fabric at the underarm curve to allow the garment to lie flat and reduce bulk. Ensure that these snips are made close to, but not right up to, the seam, as this may impair the integrity of the seam; simply snip into the seam allowances just enough to release the fabric and flatten.

①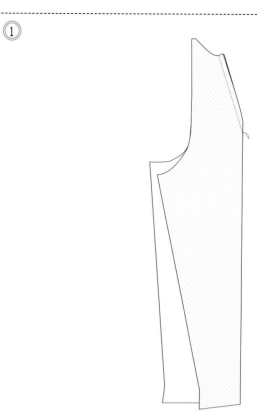

②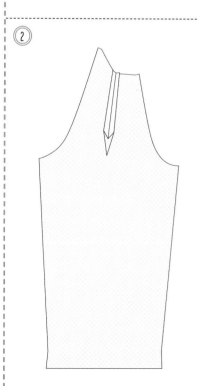

③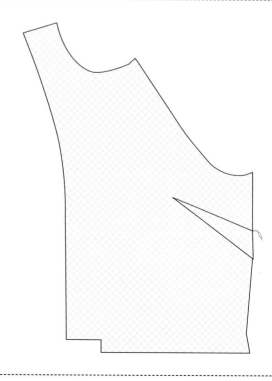

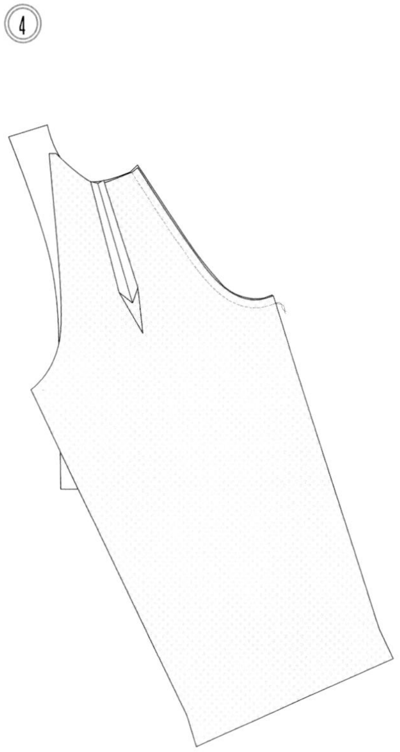
4

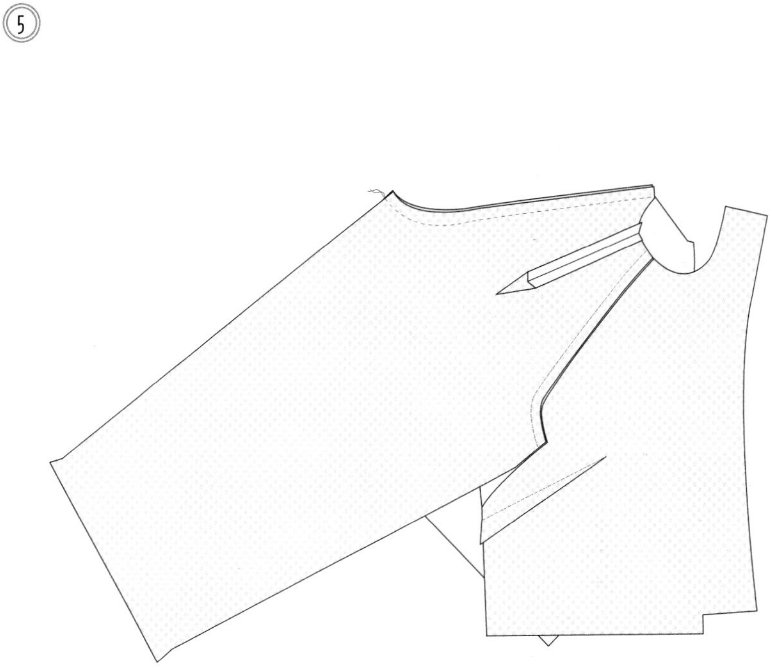
5

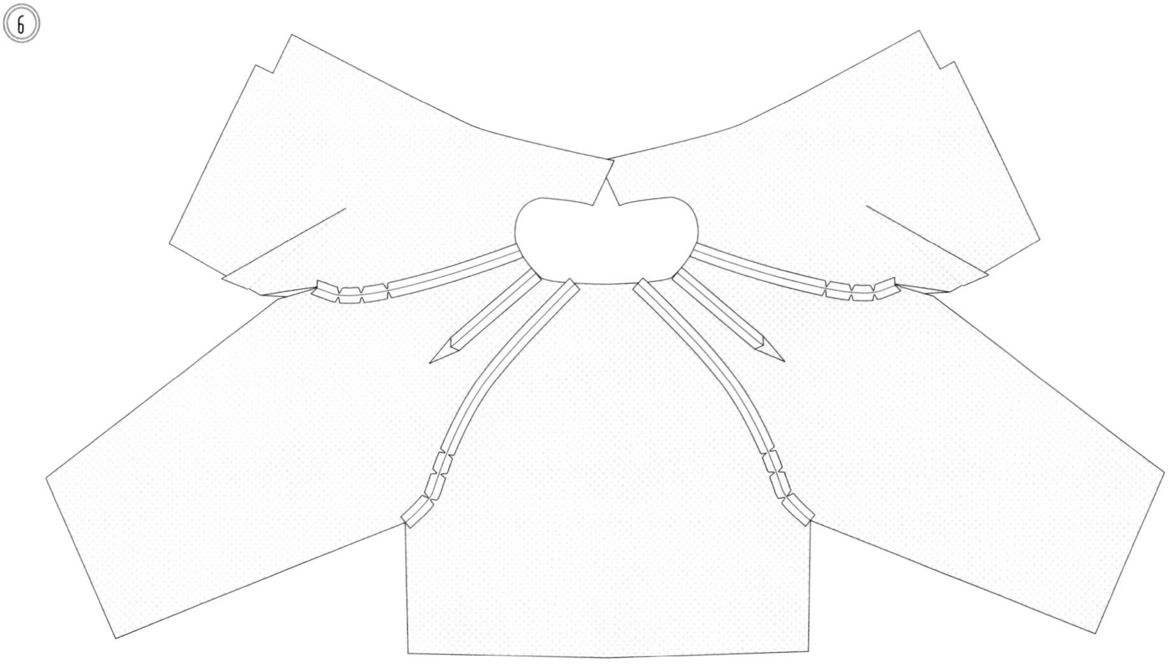
6

(7) Fold the sleeves so the right sides are facing and sew the underam seam in one. Press the seam allowances open. (8) With right sides together, join the back facing piece to the jacket front at the shoulder seams. (9) Turn the jacket to the right side. Fold the front and back neck facing into position so that right sides are facing, and machine the neckline in one. Sew the facing hem. Edgestitch the neck and grade seam allowances to reduce bulk. (10) Turn the garment to the wrong side, thus turning out the front and the neckline facing. Lightly press the facing, and fold the hem and sleeve hem into position. (11) Complete the lining following the instructions above to step 7, ensuring that the excess at the center back neck and hem is pleated. Turn back seam allowances all around. Use a row of machine basting as a guide if desired. (12) With wrong sides facing, slip the lining over the shell and hand-sew into position.

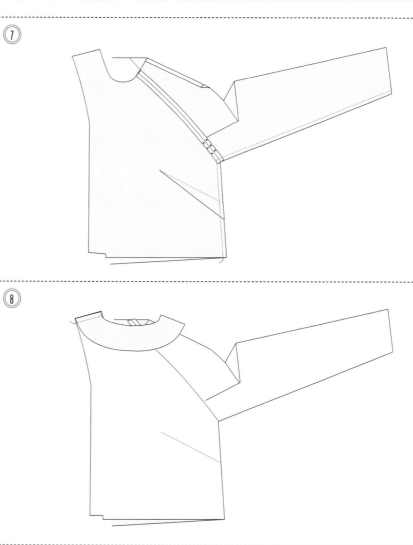

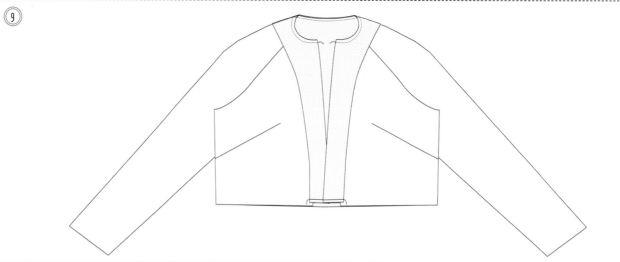

⑩

⑪

⑫

CHAPTER 6

Lingerie

The support garments and corsetry that women wore prior to the 1920s often look very restrictive to the modern eye, but they were essential to shape and mold the body and to provide support for the styles of the day. The 1920s and 1930s brought a new glamour to women's undergarments and nightwear, with lace and ribbon trims added to silk and satin fabrics in white and soft pastels. The petticoat was an important item in the 1950s to support the full skirts of the era, while firm support garments and girdles were instrumental in achieving the curvy 1950s silhouette. Support garments began to fall out of use in the 1960s and 70s as pantyhose replaced stockings and women wore more unstructured clothing. Modern women generally wear support garments and petticoats only for special-occasion dressing such as with bridal gowns or prom dresses.

Arlene Phillips floral slip.
Marisota

Support garments: 1930s on

THEN

Support garments, in their many changing forms, have been an essential part of a woman's wardrobe for centuries. From whalebone corsets through to rubber girdles, women have used their undergarments to make their clothes sit better and create a fashionable shape.

The support garments we see commonly now owe a lot to what used to be called a panty girdle. Around since the 1930s, they didn't really gain popularity until stockings started to fall out of fashion in the 1960s. They came with removable stocking clips until the 1970s, when pantyhose became the leg covering of choice for the majority of women.

Fabric innovations such as lightweight power mesh and strong Lycra fabrics mean modern support wear is much more comfortable and easier to get in and out of. Early garments were often very heavy and made from rubber with thick nylon and rayon fabrics to provide the required level of support.

WHO: Playtex was a popular manufacturer of support garments.

WHY: Support garments give a smooth shape under fitted clothing.

VARIATIONS: The waist cincher, basque, torsolette, and corsolette

SIMILAR STYLES: Bustier and petticoat, page 124

PATTERNS TO MATCH WITH: Prom dress, page 26

NOW

Alecia lingerie. *Ann Summers*

NOW

Ivory negligée. *Simply Yours*

Style and uses, then and now

FABRIC

Then: Support garments were made of heavy layers of thick, non-stretch nylon, rayon, and rubber. They gave great control but could be uncomfortable and restrictive. They were often able to stand up on their own!

Now: Lightweight fabrics with good stretch qualities, such as power mesh and Lycra, are used to provide a level of support while still allowing the wearer free movement.

LENGTH

Then: Lengths varied from a full-length corset covering the bust and hips, to a smaller waist cincher stretching from underbust to hip bone.

Now: Modern support garments vary depending on how much control is needed, and in what areas, but generally stretch from the waist to mid thigh.

STYLE

Then: Support garments came with suspenders attached to hold up stockings. They often fastened at the side with hooks and eyes, or laced up the back, making them time-consuming to put on. By the 1960s, panty girdles were more popular but specialized support garments, including waist cinchers and basques, were still worn for special occasions.

Now: Modern support garments are generally only worn for special occasions and are of the "roll-on, roll-off" style. This makes them much easier to get into, more comfortable to wear, and gives a smoother line under fitted clothing. Suspenders are rarely attached, and if they are present are usually removable. Various styles and shapes are available to work on specific problem areas or with specific dress styles, such as longer-leg versions to wear with tight skirts, or full body shapers with an attached bra to create a smooth line on the torso.

COLOR

Then: Support garments were most commonly available in soft peach or white.

Now: Support garments are generally made in flesh tones, in order to be unobtrusive under clothing, but black is now more common and some manufacturers make use of brightly colored or patterned power mesh fabrics.

MATCHED WITH

Then: Support garments were part of women's everyday attire, and taking a girl to buy her first girdle was a rite of passage. They were believed to improve posture and health.

Now: Modern support garments are designed to be worn under slinky or tight-fitting clothing for special occasions.

SEWING TIPS

- Be organized when working with multiple-piece garments. After cutting, lay out pieces in the order of construction.

- Bustier and corset shapes are often made one size smaller than the usual dress size to give a body-sculpting effect and to allow for give and stretch over time.

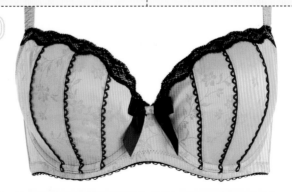

NOW

Patterned bra. *Debenhams*

Petticoats and slips: 1940s / 1950s

THEN

Deriving from the French *petite cote* ("little coat"), a petticoat was originally a padded coat worn by men under armor. From the mid-fifteenth century, the term applied to women's garments, and from then on a petticoat was always worn under women's full-length dresses.

Christian Dior's New Look of the late 1940s and early 1950s brought about a resurgence of popularity for the petticoat in the twentieth century. His full skirt styles required layers of voluminous petticoats to keep the skirt in shape; these under-layers were sometimes brightly colored and frilled for the more daring wearer. There was a certain cachet to be had in letting a flash of scarlet or bright green silk be glimpsed as glamorous postwar women swung onto buses and trains in their unsuitable but exhilarating new flowing skirts.

Petticoats have almost been phased out of fashion, but the impact they have had is still prominent. If a skirt or dress needs volume today, the petticoat is usually built into the design. Petticoats are also often required for recreating a vintage look.

WHO: Women wore petticoats under the new style of full skirts brought in by Christian Dior.

WHY: Full skirts came into vogue after the austere and severe look that was adhered to during the war years, and petticoats were required to support the skirt's shape.

VARIATIONS: Longer styles were worn, as were short and very full styles with rows upon rows of frills and lace detailing.

SIMILAR STYLES: 1920s slip, page 114; 1940s slip, page 120; bustier and petticoat, page 124

PATTERNS TO MATCH WITH: Prom dress, page 26; circle skirt, page 70

NOW

Nutmeg petticoat (www.colettepatterns.com). *Colette Patterns*

NOW

Cinnamon petticoat (www.colettepatterns.com). *Colette Patterns*

Style and uses, then and now

FABRIC

Then: Tiered, ruffled, stiffened petticoats were made from net-like crinoline and sometimes from horsehair. Nylon, chiffon, taffeta, and organdy were also used.

Now: Crinoline, taffeta, and organdy are still used, and nylon slips and half-slips are also available.

LENGTH

Then: Depending on the length of the skirts they were worn under, petticoats could be calf-length or short and almost tutu-length.

Now: The length of the petticoat still depends on the length of the skirt or dress, while half-slips are still a popular style.

STYLE

Then: Teenagers often wore shorter styles, while longer lengths had an air of rich sophistication. Often up to three petticoats were worn at any one time to achieve a full, layered effect to make the skirt stand out.

Now: The full petticoat has been replaced by simple, ungathered underskirts, although full petticoats are still worn under wedding and prom dresses.

COLORS

Then: Bright colors were employed to add a fun element that could sometimes be glimpsed under skirts. Reds, greens, and purples were often used, although traditional white was the most common color.

Now: Petticoats today are often used to streamline skirts and offer modesty where skirt fabric is thin. Nude tones as well as whites and black are often used.

MATCHED WITH

Then: Worn under poodle skirts, circle skirts, and dirndl dresses, the petticoat was a lingerie must-have during the 1950s.

Now: Worn under wedding dresses and full prom-style dresses, petticoats are regarded as special-event lingerie.

SEWING TIPS

- To speed up the construction of a full underskirt, invest in a gathering, or a ruffling and pleating foot for your sewing machine.

- Gathered or pleated lace or ribbon can be inserted between tiers during construction or added to a finished garment.

- Cut multiple layers of tulle using the circle or semicircle skirt pattern (page 70) to add to a yoke or waistband.

NOW

Tulle petticoat. *20th Century Foxy*

Slip: 1920s

GARMENT SPECS

This slip has an angular yoke that contains shaping for the bust and falls straight over the hips.
Suitable for medium- and lightweight fabrics.

STYLE VARIATIONS

The yoke section of this slip could be cut from a contrasting fabric, such as lace or broderie anglaise, or hand-embroidered prior to construction. Shorten the slip into a camisole top, or convert it into a classic flapper-style dress by adding rows of fringing. If you are adventurous, you could complete the fringing to follow the profile of the angled yoke throughout the length of the garment.

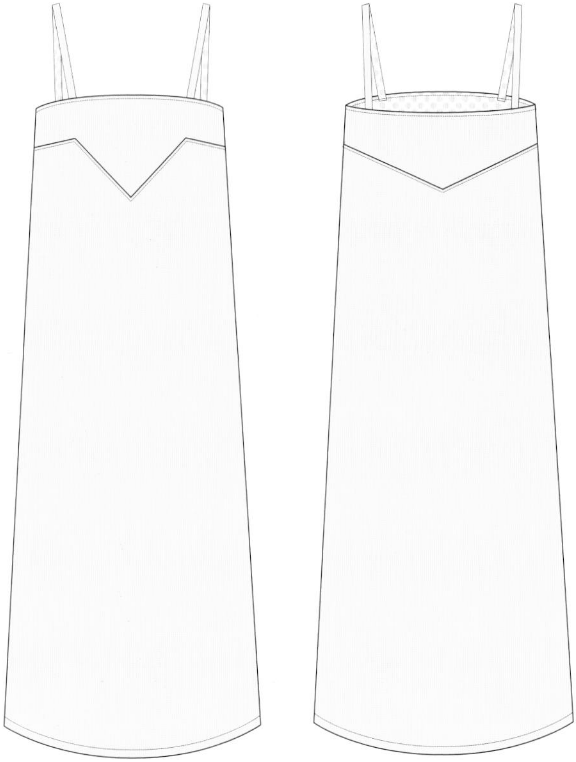

Front

Back

Sizes	S (in)	S (cm)	M (in)	M (cm)	L (in)	L (cm)	XL (in)	XL (cm)
Bust at top seam	34³⁄₁₆	86.8	36⅛	91.8	38⅛	96.8	40¹⁄₁₆	101.8
Waist 7⅞in (20cm) below top edge	33¹⁵⁄₁₆	86.2	35⅞	91.2	37⅞	96.2	39¹³⁄₁₆	101.2
Hem on seam	33¹⁵⁄₁₆	86.2	35⅞	91.2	37⅞	96.2	39¹³⁄₁₆	101.2
CB length to hem	29⅞	75.9	29⅞	75.9	29⅞	75.9	29⅞	75.9
Strap length	14½	36.8	15	38	15⁷⁄₁₆	39.2	15⅞	40.4

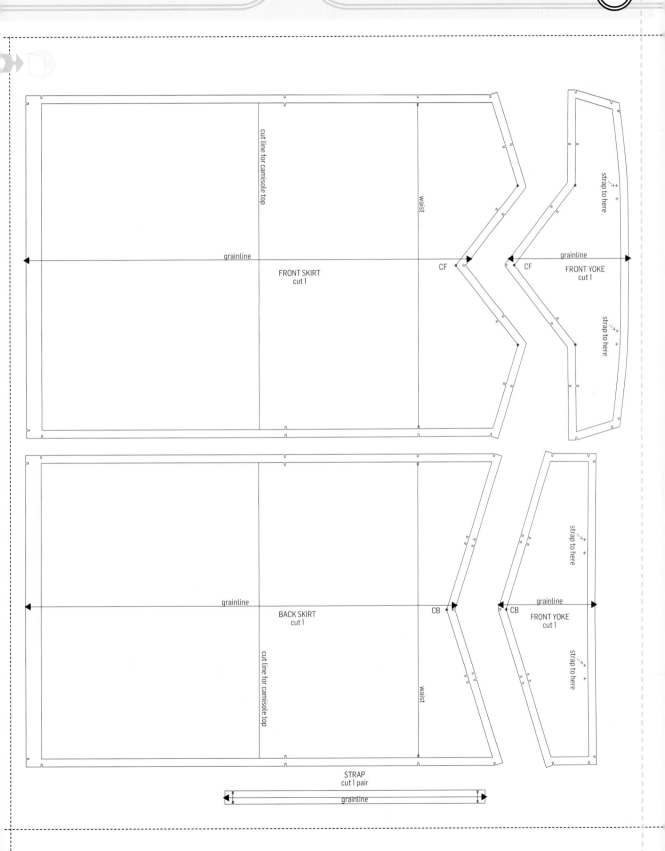

PATTERN INSTRUCTIONS

(1) With right sides together, join the front yoke to the front skirt; pin to the first drill point only and machine to this point. Ensuring the machine needle is lowered, snip the yoke section, close, but not through, the stitch line. **(2)** Keeping the machine needle through the work, pivot the yoke section and continue sewing to the CF drill hole. Keep the machine needle lowered through the work and snip into the skirt section only. Pivot the sewing and continue, completing the last apex as detailed above. **(3)** Press the seam allowance downward. To reduce bulk, miter through both layers of the upper apex. Turn the work to the right side and, using the seam as a guide, edgestitch through all layers to stabilize the seam allowance.

1

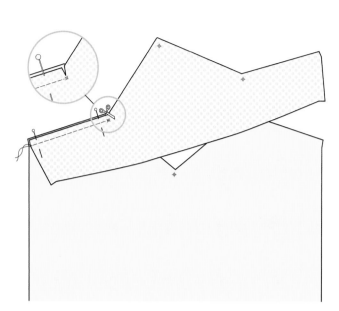

2

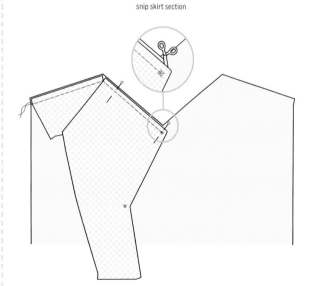

snip skirt section

3

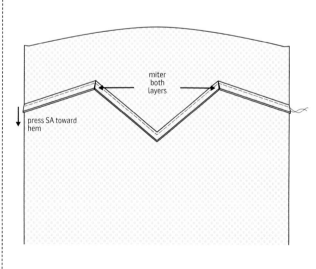

miter both layers

press SA toward hem

(4) With right sides together, sew the back yoke to the back skirt, stopping at the center back drill point. Keep the machine needle lowered, and snip the seam allowance of the skirt section only. Pivot the work and sew the other side. (5) Press the seam allowances toward the hem. Turn the work to the right side and edgestitch through all layers.
(6) Sew the side seams and press the side seams open. To create an authentic and hardwearing finish, you can finish the side seam with a welt seam: sew as for a plain seam and trim the seam allowance on the front panels (see page 167). (7) Double-turn the upper edge ¼in (6mm), pin the straps into position, and stitch all around. Finish the hem with a ¾in (2cm) single turn.

PATTERN TIP

Due to the angular nature of the yoke on this style, you should ensure that drill holes are transferred with a tailor's tack or an alternative marking technique to ensure correct matching.

4

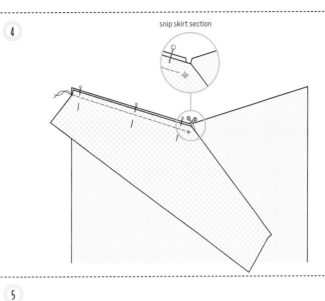

snip skirt section

5

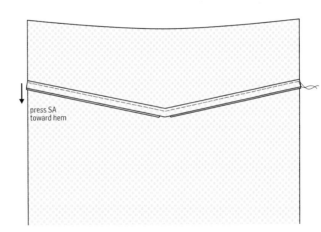

press SA toward hem

6

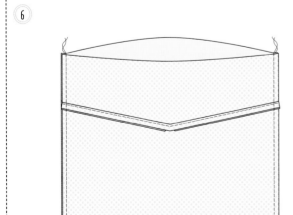

7

French knickers: 1920s

GARMENT SPECS

These 1920s-style French knickers have an elasticated waistband and hardwearing French seams. Suitable for lightweight fabrics, they can be worn with either of the camisole tops (see pages 114 and 120; cut lines to convert the slips to camisoles are indicated on both patterns).

Sizes	S (in)	S (cm)	M (in)	M (cm)	L (in)	L (cm)	XL (in)	XL (cm)
Waist on top seam	40⁷⁄₁₆	102.7	42⅜	107.7	44⅜	112.7	46⁵⁄₁₆	117.7
Hip 3¹⁵⁄₁₆in (10cm) below waistband at side seam	41⅛	104.4	43¹⁄₁₆	109.4	45¹⁄₁₆	114.4	47	119.4
Hem	26⅝	67.7	27⅝	70.2	28⅝	72.7	29⅝	75.2
Inside leg	1¾	4.5	1¾	4.5	1¾	4.5	1¾	4.5
Outside leg including waistband	9	22.9	9¼	23.5	9½	24.1	9¾	24.7
Front rise	13½	34.3	13¹³⁄₁₆	35.1	14⅛	35.9	14⁷⁄₁₆	36.7
Back rise	14⅜	36.5	14¹¹⁄₁₆	37.3	15	38.1	15⁵⁄₁₆	38.9

Front

Back

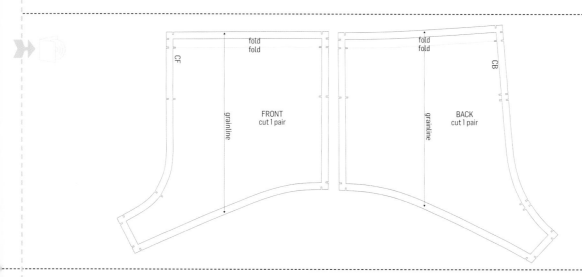

CF

fold
fold

FRONT
cut 1 pair

grainline

fold
fold

BACK
cut 1 pair

grainline

CB

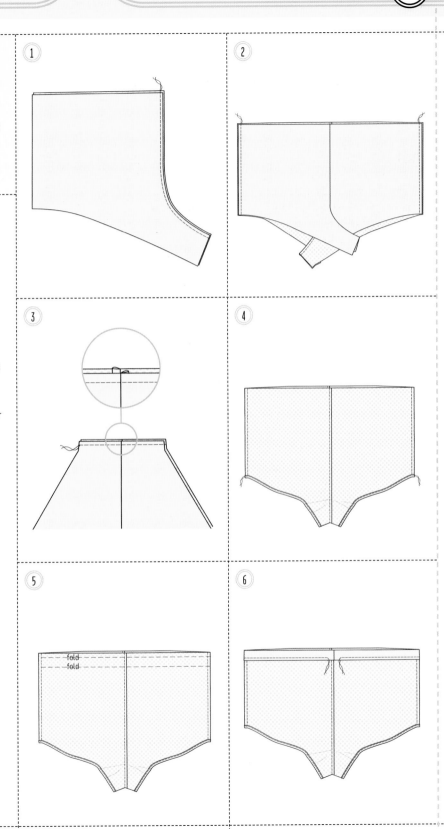

PATTERN TIP

These French knickers are constructed using a French seam (see page 164). Do not cut the notches deeper than ⅛in (3mm): this will destabilize the integrity of the seam and spoil the clean internal finish.

PATTERN INSTRUCTIONS

(1) Sew the fronts together along the center front seam. Placing wrong sides together, stitch a seam ¼in (6mm) in from the seam edge and trim back to ⅛in (3mm). Press the seam allowances open, then fold the seam right sides together. Stitch another line ¼in (6mm) in from the edge. Open the finished seam and press to one side. Repeat for the back. **(2)** With WS facing, sew the side seams using the above method. **(3)** Sew the crotch seam as above. To reduce bulk, press the seam allowances in opposite directions prior to machining. **(4)** Finish the hem on the leg edge with a ¼in (6mm) double-turn hem. **(5)** Prepare the waistband for elastic: fold and press a ½in (1.2cm) turn, followed by another 1in (2.5cm) fold, thus making a double-turned channel for the elastic. **(6)** Sew the waistband into position, leaving a gap at center back to thread the elastic through. You can machine this gap closed after inserting the elastic.

Slip: 1940s

GARMENT SPECS

This feminine 1940s-style slip falls gently from the hips and is finished with a lace trim. It is suitable for medium- and lightweight fabrics and can also be shortened into a camisole top.

Sizes	S (in)	S (cm)	M (in)	M (cm)	L (in)	L (cm)	XL (in)	XL (cm)
Back top edge	15 11/16	39.8	16 5/8	42.3	17 5/8	44.8	18 5/8	47.3
Bust	32 1/8	81.6	34 1/8	86.6	36 1/16	91.6	38 1/16	96.6
Waist 6 11/16in (17cm) below top edge	26 3/4	68	28 3/4	73	30 11/16	78	32 11/16	83
Hip 15in (38cm) below top edge	36 7/16	92.6	38 7/16	97.6	40 3/8	102.6	42 3/8	107.6
Hem on seam	57 3/8	145.8	59 3/8	150.8	61 5/16	155.8	63 5/16	160.8
Strap length	15 1/4	38.8	15 3/4	40	16 1/4	41.2	16 11/16	42.4
CB length	33 1/2	85.1	33 1/2	85.1	33 1/2	85.1	33 1/2	85.1

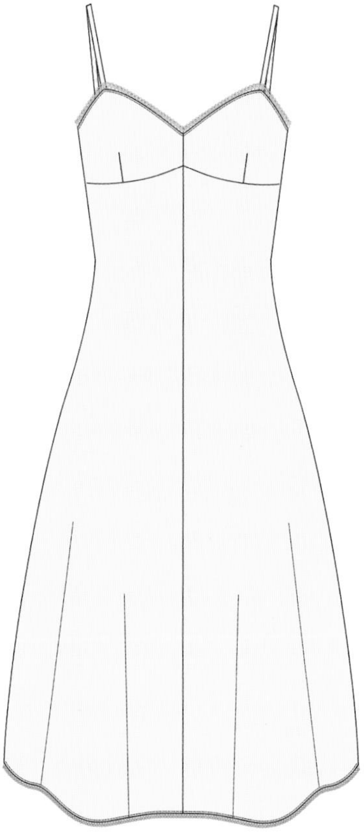

Front

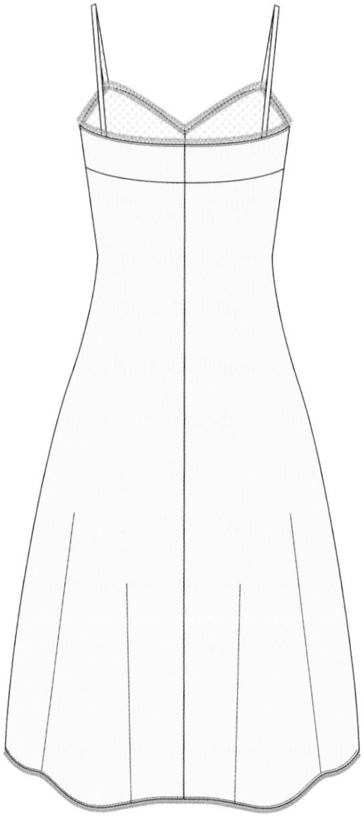

Back

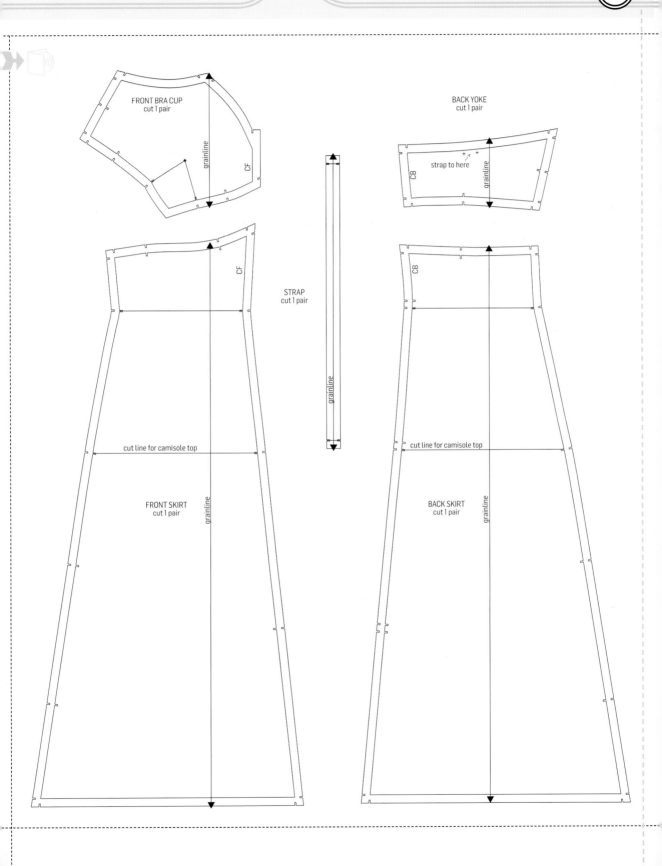

FRONT BRA CUP
cut 1 pair

grainline

CF

BACK YOKE
cut 1 pair

CB

strap to here

grainline

STRAP
cut 1 pair

grainline

CF

CB

cut line for camisole top

cut line for camisole top

FRONT SKIRT
cut 1 pair

grainline

BACK SKIRT
cut 1 pair

grainline

PATTERN TIP

Before releasing the pattern pieces from the fabric, snip all the notches and mark the drill holes with a tailor's tack.

PATTERN INSTRUCTIONS

(1) Sew the bust dart on each front bra cup and trim the dart down to ½in (1.2cm). Press the seam allowance toward the side seam. With right sides together, matching notches, sew one bust cup to one front skirt. Repeat for the other side. Sew one back yoke to one back skirt. Repeat for the other side. Press the seam allowances toward the hem. **(2)** With right sides together, sew the fronts together along CF. Repeat for the back and press the seams open. **(3)** With right sides together, sew the side seams and press them open. Turn the work to the right side. **(4)** Finish the uppermost edge with lace or braid: fold back ½in (1.2cm) at the center back and pin lace in position to CF only. **(5)** At the apex of the bust cup, pivot the work, keeping the machine needle lowered, and make a small tuck in the lace. When you reach the CF, keep the machine needle down and pivot the work; you can now pin the rest of the trim into position. Continue sewing to center back, overlapping the lace for a short distance. Press the lace upward, with the seam allowance toward the hem. **(6)** Prepare the lace strap to the required length, folding the lower edge, and pin into position. Stitch the lace at the center front to create a mitered edge. **(7)** Turn the garment to the right side and topstitch through all layers, securing the strap at the front and the back. Finish the hem with lace using the above method.

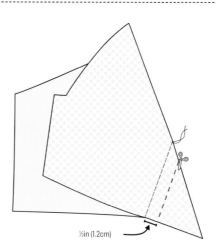

1

½in (1.2cm)

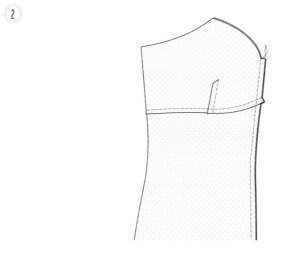

2

3

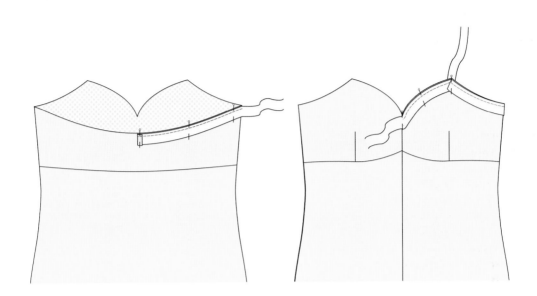

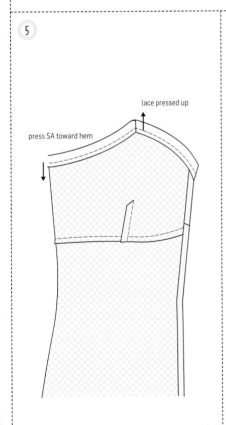

press SA toward hem

lace pressed up

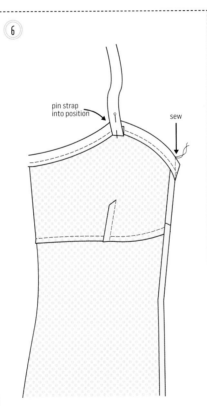

pin strap into position

sew

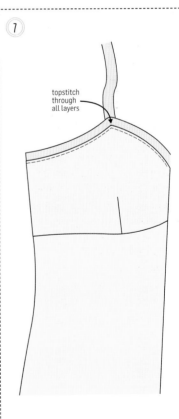

topstitch through all layers

Bustier and petticoat: 1950s

GARMENT SPECS

This full-skirted petticoat and close-fitting bustier will provide support to a circular-cut skirt or dress but, with the right fabric, could also be worn as outerwear. The design is suitable for a variety of fabrics; consider making the lower tiers of the petticoat from dress net.

Sizes	S (in)	S (cm)	M (in)	M (cm)	L (in)	L (cm)	XL (in)	XL (cm)
Bust	31⅞	81	33⅞	86	35¹³⁄₁₆	91	37¹³⁄₁₆	96
Waist on seam	25³⁄₁₆	64	27³⁄₁₆	69	29⅛	74	31⅛	79
Lower seam of the first tier	35½	90.2	37½	95.2	39⁷⁄₁₆	100.2	41⁷⁄₁₆	105.2
Hem on seam	297¼	755	299³⁄₁₆	760	301³⁄₁₆	765	303⅛	770
CB length	29¹³⁄₁₆	75.7	29¹³⁄₁₆	75.7	29¹³⁄₁₆	75.7	29¹³⁄₁₆	75.7

Front

Back

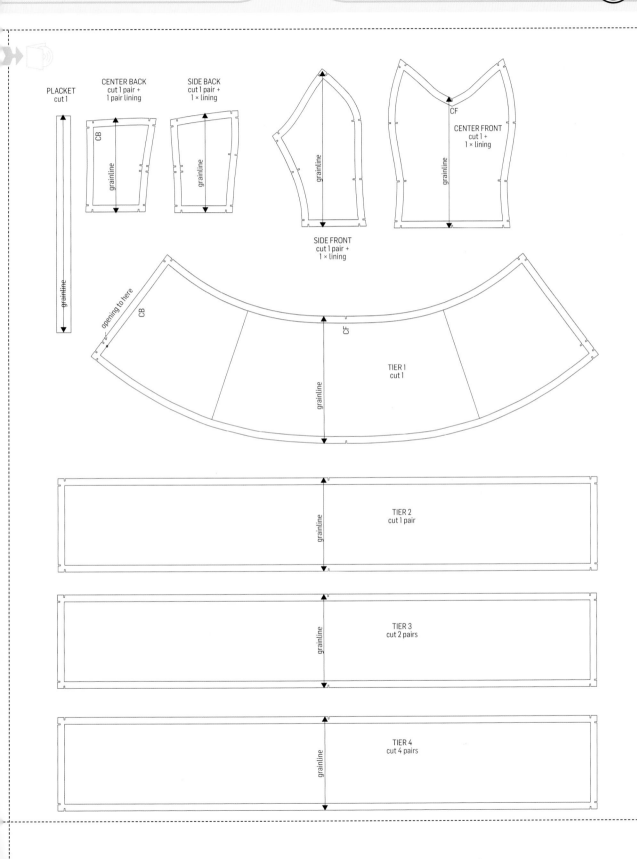

PLACKET
cut 1

CENTER BACK
cut 1 pair +
1 pair lining

CB

grainline

SIDE BACK
cut 1 pair +
1 × lining

grainline

grainline

grainline

SIDE FRONT
cut 1 pair +
1 × lining

CF

CENTER FRONT
cut 1 +
1 × lining

grainline

grainline

opening to here

CB

CF

grainline

TIER 1
cut 1

grainline

TIER 2
cut 1 pair

grainline

TIER 3
cut 2 pairs

grainline

TIER 4
cut 4 pairs

PATTERN TIP

This garment contains a number of duplicate pieces; organize the garment pieces prior to sewing, stacking pieces that will be machined together to avoid confusion during construction.

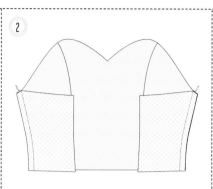

PATTERN INSTRUCTIONS

(1) With right sides together, sew the side front panel to the center front, then repeat for the other side. Press the seam allowances open, taking care not to flatten the bust shaping with heavy-handed pressing. (2) Placing RS together, sew the side back panels to the side front, and press the seam allowances open. (3) Again, with RS facing, sew the center back panels to the side back panels. Press the seam allowances open and set aside. Repeat for the lining. (4) Attach the boning to the lining, using the zipper foot. Ensure the boning does not extend over the sewing line. If you are not using boning with a ready-prepared casing, cover the boning with a suitable ribbon or tape. (5) With RS facing, sew the lining and outer together, leaving the waist edge open. Understitch the seam allowances of the upper edge to the lining only, and grade seam allowances to reduce bulk. Turn to right side, carefully press, and set aside. If you would prefer a zipper opening, sew the upper edge only, understitch, and join to the skirt before inserting the zipper, treating the lining piece as a facing and finishing the facing zipper edge by hand.

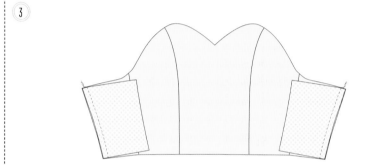

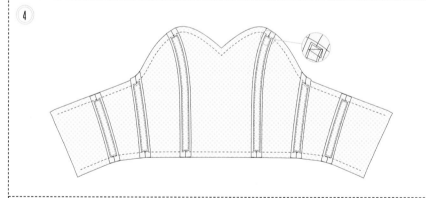

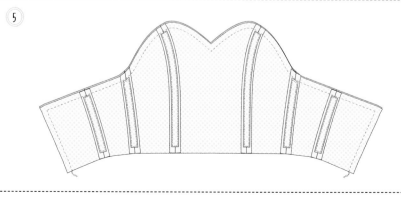

(6) To prepare the skirt, set tier 1 aside for now, and with RS together sew 2 × second tier panels together at side seams, pressing the seam allowances open. Leave the center back seam open. Repeat for 4 × third tier and 8 × fourth tier. Gather or pleat the upper edges of tier 4 to match the hem of tier 3, using a gather or pleat ratio of 2:1. With RS facing, sew the tiers together. Join tier 3 to tier 2 using the above method. You can now join the gathered upper edge of tier 2 to the curved lower edge of tier 1. (7) Placing RS together, sew the center back seam of the skirt from hem to drill hole, ensuring the seam allowance on each tier is pushed toward the waist edge. Snip the seam allowance close, but not through to the stitch line, and trim the opening seam allowances down to ¼in (6mm). Miter the bottom edge. (8) Finish the opening with a continuous lapped placket. Spread the opening and, with RS together, machine the placket along the opening using a ¼in (6mm) seam allowance. Fold the placket over to WS and, tucking the raw edge under, machine or hand-stitch into position. To stop the placket from turning to the right side, stitch across the bottom edge at 45 degrees. (9) To join the bustier to the petticoat, with RS together, sew the outer to the petticoat along the waist edge, ensuring the lining of the waist edge remains free and is not caught during stitching. Press seam allowances upward, and machine or hand-stitch the lining into position at the waist to hide the raw edges. Add hook-and-eye tape to center back and finish the hem on the petticoat.

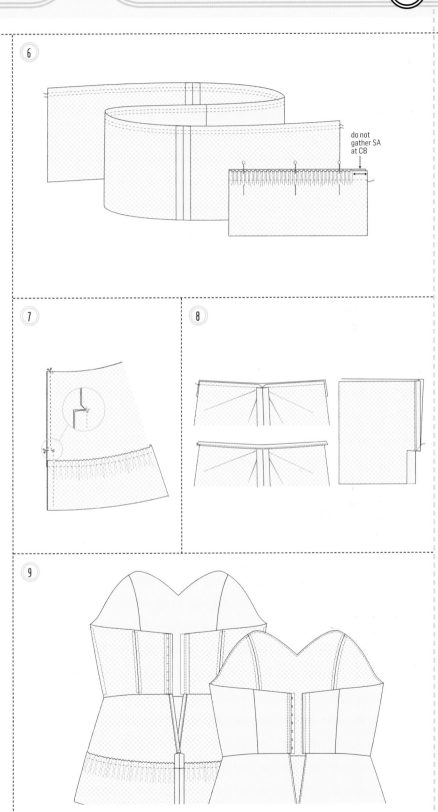

do not gather SA at CB

CHAPTER 7

Headwear and gloves

Headwear and gloves have always served practical purposes, particularly for protecting wearers from cold. However, various accessories have enjoyed their time in the fashion spotlight. The cloche hat is an emblem of the free-spirited 1920s flapper, while elbow-length white gloves were often teamed with the elegant floor-length evening gowns of the 1930s. In the 1940s and 1950s both men and women nearly always wore hats to complete an outfit, while the 1960s saw new looks in headgear including the primly chic pillbox hat, forever associated with Jackie Kennedy, and the baker-boy cap that set off a bobbed haircut so well. Today women embrace accessories of all sorts, and carefully chosen hats, scarfs, and gloves are all key items to pull an outfit together.

Micro pom-pom fez.
Ann-Marie Faulkner Millinery

Gloves: *1920s to 1960s*

THEN

Although always the same basic shape, gloves come in a range of fabrics, colors, and lengths, for a variety of uses. Gloves were a fashion item and a status symbol for centuries, and considered an essential piece of daywear for women up until the 1960s. White or cream cotton gloves were popular for daywear, and crochet versions were available for summer wear.

From the 1970s onward, gloves were generally made in wool or leather and worn for warmth, rather than as a fashion accessory, during the day. For eveningwear, gloves have remained popular into the modern day, available in wrist, elbow, and opera length. Made in satin or a fine fabric such as kid leather or suede, they add a touch of elegance to a formal outfit.

WHO: Dents and Pittards were popular glove manufacturers.

WHY: They add elegance to an outfit.

VARIATIONS: Fingerless gloves or mittens

SIMILAR STYLES: N/A

PATTERNS TO MATCH WITH: Prom dress, page 26; pillbox hat, page 138

NOW

Tweed gloves. *Marks & Spencer*

NOW

Teal bow gloves. M&Co

Style and uses, then and now

FABRIC

Then: Cotton was more affordable than leather, and popular for summer wear. Many women owned a pair of fine leather gloves for special occasions. For evening-wear, gloves made of kid leather or silk added a touch more glamor.

Now: For daywear, modern gloves are generally made in warmer fabrics such as wool or leather. Longer evening gloves are available in stretch satin. This ensures a good fit and makes the gloves much easier to put on and take off than those made from a tight-fighting, nonstretch fabric.

LENGTH

Then: Gloves for daywear were often wrist length, while evening gloves stretched over the elbow.

Now: Gloves are still available in lengths from wrist to over the elbow for evening.

STYLE

Then: Clean gloves for day wear were the mark of a lady and an essential part of a woman's wardrobe.

Now: During the day modern gloves are most often worn for warmth. They continue to be popular accessories for evening and formal wear, particularly in longer, over-the-elbow opera length, and are often worn with bridal, prom, or debutante gowns.

COLORS

Then: Gloves were worn in a color to coordinate with a woman's outfit and possibly dyed to match shoes, hats, or handbags.

Now: Black or white are the most popular shades for formal gloves, worn to contrast with the dress—black with a white dress or white with black. They can also be worn in a bright hue, such as red or fuchsia, to add color and drama, or to coordinate with the shade of the gown.

MATCHED WITH

Then: Gloves were a feature of both day- and eveningwear, teamed with suits or summer dresses and with evening gowns.

Now: Choose the length of your gloves based on the length of the sleeves on your dress. Sleeveless gowns should be worn with full-length opera gloves, dresses with short sleeves look best worn with an elbow or gauntlet length, and full-length sleeves can be teamed with wrist-length gloves.

SEWING TIPS

- Sewing gloves on a domestic sewing machine can be tricky; change to a narrow foot or sew by hand.

- Use a wedge-shaped needle to sew leather.

- Unpick an existing pair of gloves and trace onto pattern paper to make a pattern.

NOW

Satin gloves. (Model's own)

The printed scarf: 1920s on

THEN

The printed scarf has been a prominent fashion feature in each decade of the twentieth century. In the 1920s and 1930s, long Deco-print tasseled scarfs were worn wrapped around the neck, while shorter versions of the accessory layered up in a formal masculine style. However, the printed scarf really came into its own in the 1940s, when Hermès became synonymous with square scene-print "postcard" styles.

It was around this time that scarfs began to be worn in the hair, most famously by Land Girls serving in World War II. American rockabillies in the 1950s also appropriated the look, wearing leopard print, gingham, and polka-dot scarfs in their carefully coiffured curls. Longer lengths and Eastern-inspired patterns became part of the glamorous bohemian look of the 1960s and 1970s, while ostentatious prints characterized the 1980s.

Vintage-style printed square scarfs are again in demand with those recreating 1950s fashions, while longer cotton styles are wrapped loosely around the neck for a more casual look.

WHO: Associated with Hermès, whose scarfs have been worn by royalty including Queen Elizabeth II and Grace Kelly, later Princess Grace of Monaco.

WHY: Versatile, practical, and fun. Often worn as a status symbol.

VARIATIONS: Larger shawls and sarongs worn as cover-ups were particularly popular during the 1970s bohemian period.

SIMILAR STYLES: Turban, page 134

PATTERNS TO MATCH WITH: Wide-legged pants, page 82

NOW

Polka-dot headscarf. (Model's own)

NOW

Palmleaf scarf. *Plümo*

Style and uses, then and now

FABRIC

Then: Silk has long been the preferred material for printed scarfs, but cotton was also used for daytime looks.

Now: As well as silk and cotton, polyester and nylon are used to produce printed scarfs.

LENGTH

Then: In the 1920s, long tasseled scarfs were worn wrapped around the neck, to be replaced by square styles up until the 1960s and 1970s, when the glamorous bohemian look saw vast swathes of material come into fashion.

Now: Vintage-inspired square scarfs are currently enjoying a fashion revival, worn at the neck or tied in the hair, with longer scarfs worn wrapped loosely around the neck.

STYLE

Then: Deco and postcard-scene motifs; leopard, fruit, and floral prints; Eastern-inspired patterns and nautical themes have all appeared on scarfs from the 1920s to the 1980s.

Now: Postcard-scene motifs on square silk scarfs are once again popular with those favoring the retro look, while traditional florals, as well as trend-led leopard, skull, and animal motif prints are a popular choice for longer styles.

COLORS

Then: The continued popularity of the printed scarf has much to do with the wide variety of colors and designs used in new designs to fit the fashions of each decade.

Now: Pastel florals, vibrant Eastern-inspired dyes, neon accents, and rich animal-print scarfs are among the styles recently championed on Fashion Week runways and in mainstream fashion stores.

MATCHED WITH

Then: Worn with everything from dresses and trouser suits to Land Girl dungarees.

Now: Proving that the printed scarf remains one of fashion's most versatile accessories, today's vintage and new scarfs are worn with outfits varying from formal dresses to casual jeans-and-top combinations and also as decorative additions to handbags. Scarf prints even appeared on dresses, tops, shirts, and skirts in recent spring/summer collections.

SEWING TIPS

- Add lace, crochet, or fringe edging to an existing scarf.
- Add a scalloped edge using the technique described on page 182.
- Sew scarfs together to create a slip petticoat or kimono jacket.

NOW

Polka-dot headscarf. (Model's own)

The turban: 1920s on

THEN

Traditionally made from a long scarf of fine linen, cotton, or silk and worn wound around the head, the turban has been periodically popular as an item of headwear throughout the 20th century.

Turbans first became a fashion statement for Western women in the early twentieth century, when French designer Paul Poiret brought out turbans teamed with Oriental-inspired harem pants and tunics. During the 1930s, the turban became a popular style of hat, reconstructed by milliners into the somewhat pointed shape with which fashion is now familiar.

Turbans have gone in and out of fashion sporadically over the decades, being briefly popular for both day and nightwear in the 1930s, 1960s, and 1980s; 2007 also saw a revival in the turban, with Eastern-influenced designs seen on many runway collections, most notably Prada.

WHO: French designer Paul Poiret introduced turbans into the fashion mainstream.

WHY: Made from an assortment of versatile fabrics, the turban was a new way to wear headgear.

VARIATION: There are various ways to tie turbans, each exhibiting a different look. Turbans could also be decorated with brooches and feathers for extra sophistication.

SIMILAR STYLES: Printed scarf, page 132

PATTERNS TO MATCH WITH: Drop-waisted dress, page 22

NOW

Sequin turban. *Accessorize*

Style and uses, then and now

FABRICS

Then: Made from cotton for everyday wear and satins and silks for evening. Muslin and organdy were also popular.

Now: Silk and silk satins are a common choice, with turbans often regarded as a high-fashion accessory.

LENGTH

Then: Traditional turbans could measure anything up to 23 feet (7m) long to achieve height when wound around the head.

Now: Traditional styles can still be very long, while styles seen on the runway are often ready-made into the turban shape.

STYLE

Then: In the 1940s, the turban was often worn as a simple safety device to prevent the wearer's hair from getting caught in factory machinery. It also usefully disguised unkempt hair. By the 1960s, the style had become more decadent and associated with affluence.

Now: Turbans worn for fashion effect nowadays mostly come ready-made, so the wearer can simply slip it on over their hair.

COLORS

Then: Colors were bright during the 1960s, with red, blue, green, and checkered styles all popular.

Now: Turbans come in an array of colors, with metallic gold and silver styles often favored.

MATCHED WITH:

Then: Worn with silk ribbon decoration, fur stoles, and high-neck-collar coats, the turban lent the wearer an air of sophistication.

Now: Taking inspiration from the turban's traditional provenance, the style has most recently been paired with harem pants and cropped jackets.

NOW

Chic turban. *Topshop*

NOW

Hand-knitted turban. (Model's own)

SEWING TIPS

- A turban-style headband can be constructed from turned-out sections of jersey. Take two sections of jersey of double the desired width and half the head measurement. Add seam allowance turnings and turn out, leaving one short edge open. Fold both sections in half and interlink the two pieces. Sew the unfinished edges together to complete.

The pillbox hat: 1960s

THEN

Pillbox hats are small hats that have straight, upright sides, a flat crown, and no brim. Historically, pillbox hats were worn as military headgear with a chinstrap. They became fashionable in the 1930s, although it was Jacqueline Kennedy, the First Lady of the United States, who popularized pillbox hats in the early 1960s. Classically, the pillbox hat is small enough that it can be pinned on the head. Placing the pillbox hat at different angles, such as at the crown or further back on the head, achieves different looks, from cutesy to dramatic, and the simple shape helps to accentuate facial features in a gentle way.

Pillbox hats were often worn as accessories with bouffant hairdos, which were popular in the 1960s. They were worn in plain colors for a classic, understated look, or were dressed up with embellishments for a dressier look using veils, pins, beads, jewels, braiding, ribbons, and flowers.

WHO: Cristóbal Balenciaga is credited with designing the pillbox hat in the early 1950s. Oleg Cassini was Jacqueline Kennedy's main designer and is credited with designing her signature pillbox hats.

WHY: The pillbox hat was regarded as a symbol of prim and proper high fashion, influenced by Jacqueline Kennedy's style.

VARIATIONS: Pillbox hats were worn plain or were dressed up with embellishments.

SIMILAR STYLES: Turban, page 134

PATTERNS TO MATCH WITH: Box-pleated skirt, page 66; box jacket, page 102

NOW

Silver glass pillbox. *Ann-Marie Faulkner Millinery*

Style and uses, then and now

FABRIC

Then: Pillbox hats were typically made from sturdy material such as felt.

Now: All sorts of fabrics are used to make pillbox hats today, from cotton through to velvet and faux fur.

LENGTH

Then: Pillbox hats in the 1960s were small, round, and either plain or decorated with stylish embellishments.

Now: Modern styles are a lot more adventurous, and are available in a variety of shapes and colors.

STYLE

Then: Pillbox hats were available in many different sizes. Some fit the head like a regular hat, but many were small and designed to sit on the top of the head. In shape they were circular or oval.

Now: The same sizes are made, but pillbox hats today are available in a wider variety of shapes, including hearts and teardrops.

COLORS

Then: For more formal affairs, such as weddings and dinners, solid colors were worn. The most important thing was to make sure pillbox hats coordinated with the color of the wearer's outfit.

Now: Pillbox hats are available in a huge variety of colors today and are often worn as statement pieces (rather than blending in with the outfit), featuring bold and adventurous patterns and trims.

MATCHED WITH

Then: Jacqueline Kennedy often wore pillbox hats as accessories with buttoned wool suits and a bouffant hairdo. They were also commonly worn in the 1960s with shift and A-line dresses, and also with veils as wedding attire.

Now: For a classic look, match your pillbox hat with a skirt suit or shift dress, tweed jacket, structured handbag, heels, and a string of pearls. The key to pulling off the classic look is to make your pillbox hat match your outfit. Alternatively, go for a plainer outfit with a statement pillbox hat in a bold color or pattern. For weddings, pair a pillbox hat with a short veil with a fitted gown.

SEWING TIPS

- For a professional look, you can purchase a hat base from a millinery supplier instead of using buckram.

- Experiment with the size and shape of your hat: try an oval, teardrop, or heart-shaped hat.

- Experiment with embellishments such as beads, netting, features, and patches.

- If you choose a lightweight fabric, use a heavy interfacing. This will ensure that your hat is strong enough to stand up on its own.

NOW

Pillbox fascinator. (Model's own)

Pillbox hat: 1960s

GARMENT SPECS

This pillbox hat can be decorated in a variety of ways or left plain.
Consider using velvet or woolen fabrics. The instructions below
describe the sewing instructions for a circular bias-brim hat,
but we also provide a pattern for an oval straight-cut hat.
The instructions for construction are interchangeable.

Round Pillbox (one size)	(in)	(cm)
Circumference	23¹³⁄₁₆	60.5
Height	2¾	7
Oval Pillbox (one size)	**(in)**	**(cm)**
Circumference	20¹⁄₁₆	51
Height	2¾	7

Plain

WIth lace

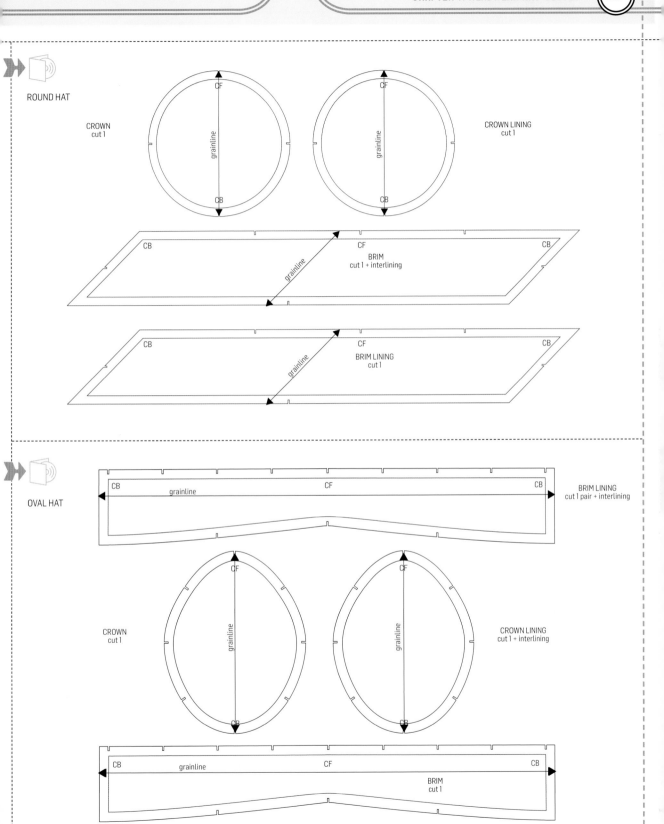

PATTERN TIP

This hat requires interlining to provide structure. Use buckram if possible; otherwise you may need to improvise with whatever materials are to hand.

PATTERN INSTRUCTIONS

(1) With right sides together, sew the hat brim along the center back seam. (2) Press with the seam allowance open and trim any excess allowances. (3) With right sides facing, sew the crown and brim together, taking great care to match notches. Try to avoid flattening the pieces as you sew them together; this may create unsightly puckers as excess fabric is caught during sewing. Instead, try to keep a curved shape as you feed the piece through the machine. Understitch the seam allowances to the brim only. (4) Miter the seam allowances to remove excess fabric if necessary and turn to the right side. Steam the hat shape. (5) Repeat steps 1 to 4 to construct the hat lining. (6) With wrong sides together, place the lining into the hat. (7) Lay a strip of ribbon or braid to the outside of the hat and pin it into position. Sandwich a piece of elastic between the main hat and the braid and edgestitch it into place through all layers. (8) Turn the braid to the wrong side, trim the elastic, and handstitch into position. (9) Decorate as desired. This illustration shows loosely gathered netting and a rolled piece of ribbon. More decoration ideas are suggested on page 180.

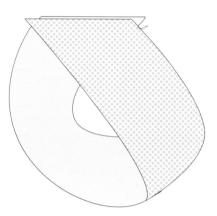

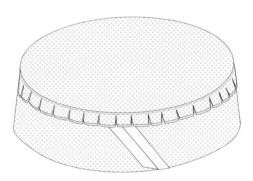

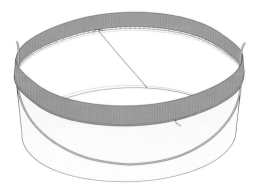

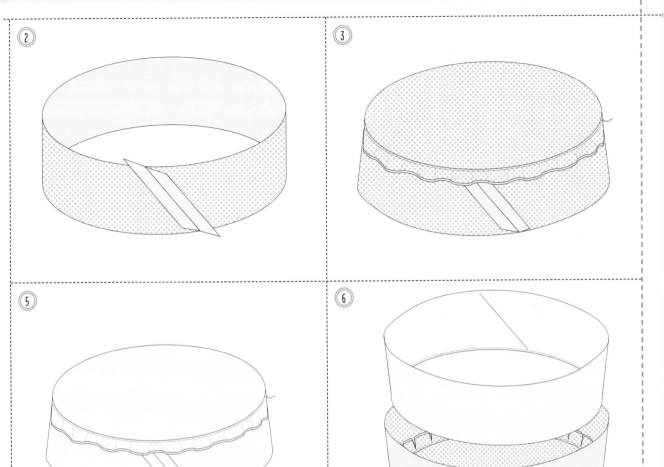

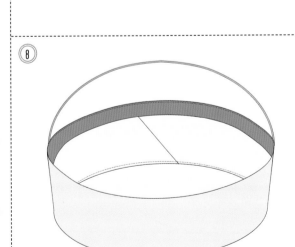

CHAPTER 8
Dressmaking basics

This chapter covers useful techniques for creating your own vintage-inspired pieces. It outlines the stages you need to work through before beginning the construction of your garment, from understanding the terms and symbols used in commercial dressmaking patterns through adjusting a pattern to meet your needs and measurements, to the last essential stage: cutting out and marking fabric in the most efficient and cost-effective way.

Marabou shrug. *AW12 Womenswear Model Images*

Pattern annotation

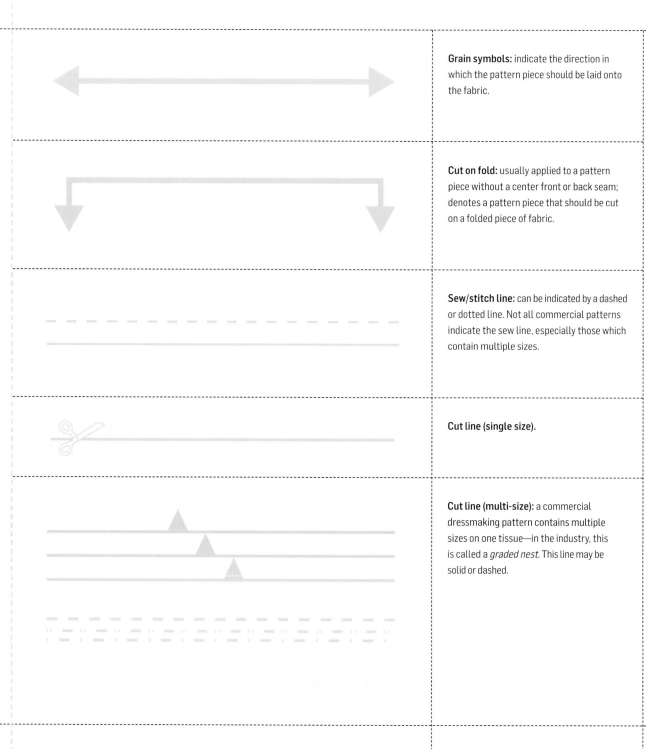

Grain symbols: indicate the direction in which the pattern piece should be laid onto the fabric.

Cut on fold: usually applied to a pattern piece without a center front or back seam; denotes a pattern piece that should be cut on a folded piece of fabric.

Sew/stitch line: can be indicated by a dashed or dotted line. Not all commercial patterns indicate the sew line, especially those which contain multiple sizes.

Cut line (single size).

Cut line (multi-size): a commercial dressmaking pattern contains multiple sizes on one tissue—in the industry, this is called a *graded nest*. This line may be solid or dashed.

Pleat symbols: these indicate pleat position and pleat fold direction.

Buttonhole position.

Button position.

Drill hole: indicates precise matching or construction points such as the apex of a dart. Mark with chalk or tailor tack.

Notches: solid triangles are often marked on commercial dressmaker's patterns to indicate the positions of notches on individual seams that need to be lined up during construction. A double triangle indicates a back pattern piece. Throughout this book notches are indicated with an open rectangle; their function is the same.

Standard measurements

Begin by measuring the bust across the fullest part. Allow the tape to rise up about 1 inch (2.5cm) at the center back; if the tape drops, the measurement will decrease and the resulting measurement will be too tight. Compare the measurements you have with those on the chart to find those nearest in bust size; if store-bought clothes generally fit well, you may find that the average measurements give successful results. If your measurements differ significantly from those in the chart below, you may need to adjust the patterns (see pages 148–155).

 NATURAL POSTURE

Ask the person you are measuring to stand naturally, looking forward. If they do not usually have an upright posture, do not mask their true figure with one during measuring.

Sizes		S (in)	S (cm)	M (in)	M (cm)	L (in)	L (cm)	XL (in)	XL (cm)
1	Bust	32¹¹⁄₁₆	83.00	34⅝	88.00	36⅝	93.00	38⁹⁄₁₆	98.00
2	Waist	25⁹⁄₁₆	65.00	27⁹⁄₁₆	70.00	29½	75.00	31½	80.00
3	Hip	35¹⁄₁₆	89.00	37	94.00	39	99.00	40¹⁵⁄₁₆	104.00
4	Back width	12⁹⁄₁₆	31.90	13⁹⁄₁₆	34.40	14½	36.90	15½	39.40
5	Shoulder	4¹¹⁄₁₆	11.95	4¹³⁄₁₆	12.25	4¹⁵⁄₁₆	12.55	5¹⁄₁₆	12.85
6	Neck size	14⅛	35.80	14⁹⁄₁₆	37.00	15¹⁄₁₆	38.20	15½	39.40
7	Upper arm	10½	26.60	11³⁄₁₆	28.40	11⅞	30.20	12⅝	32.00
8	Nape to waist	15⅞	40.40	16⅛	41.00	16⅜	41.60	16⅝	42.20
9	Armhole depth	7¹⁵⁄₁₆	20.20	8¼	21.00	8⁹⁄₁₆	21.80	8⅞	22.60
10	Waist to knee	22¹³⁄₁₆	57.90	23¹⁄₁₆	58.50	23¼	59.10	23¼	59.10
11	Waist to hip	8⅛	20.60	8⅛	20.60	8⅛	20.60	8⅛	20.60
12	Waist to floor	40¹¹⁄₁₆	103.40	40¹⁵⁄₁₆	104.00	41³⁄₁₆	104.60	41⁷⁄₁₆	105.20
13	Body rise	10¹³⁄₁₆	27.40	11	28.00	11¼	28.60	11½	29.20
14	Sleeve length	22⅞	58.10	23¹⁄₁₆	58.50	23³⁄₁₆	58.90	23⅜	59.30

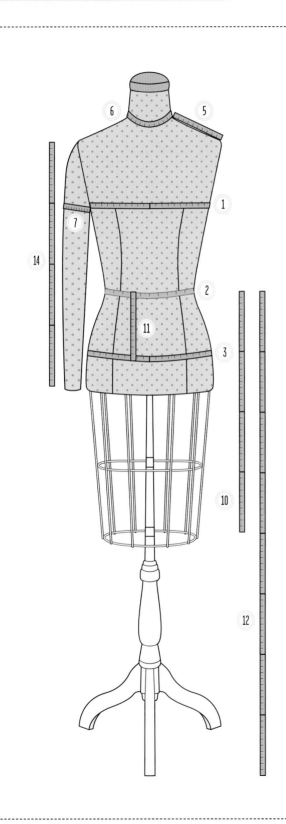

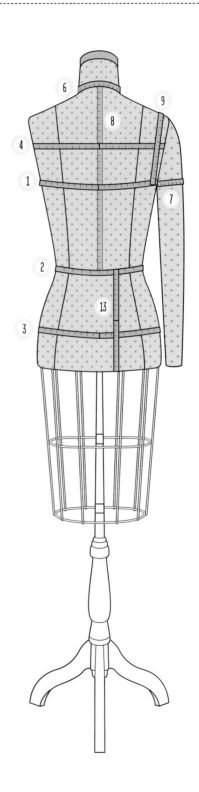

Adjusting patterns

You can make initial adjustments to length and width on your pattern before cutting out your fitting muslin; other necessary alterations may become apparent only when the garment is tried on for the first time. Place the first muslin on the body or dress form with the right sides toward the body and the seam allowances outermost; this allows easy access to unpick and re-pin alterations.

Length

You can adjust the length of a pattern by extending or overlapping the pattern across its entire width. These diagrams show how to adjust the length of: **(1)** sleeves, **(2)** a skirt, and **(3)** a dress/bodice. The dress/bodice block shows how to adjust both above and below the waist; after comparing your measurements to the pattern you may find only one of these adjustments is necessary (that is, either above or below the waist).

1

Pattern adjustment position

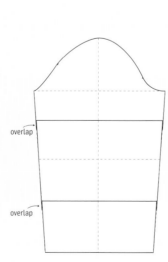

overlap

overlap

Shorten

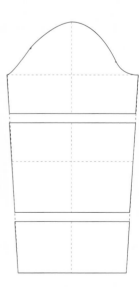

Lengthen

2

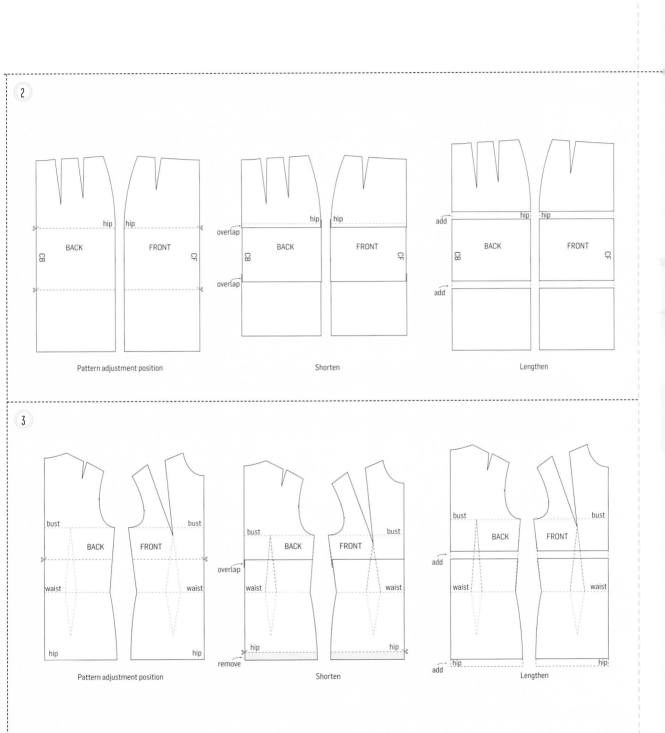

Pattern adjustment position

Shorten

Lengthen

3

Pattern adjustment position

Shorten

Lengthen

Width

If you are making width adjustments to a style with more than one front or back panel, allocate the width equally between all the pattern pieces in the design. You can add a basic adjustment of 1 inch (2.5cm) or less to the pattern's side seams. If you require extra width only at the waist or hips, you need only add to these parts of the pattern.

Do not make width adjustments through the armhole or neckline, as this will compromise your pattern and impair its fit. Whenever you make any alteration to your pattern, you should also adjust any neighboring pattern pieces, such as facings, side seams, or waist seams, as necessary.

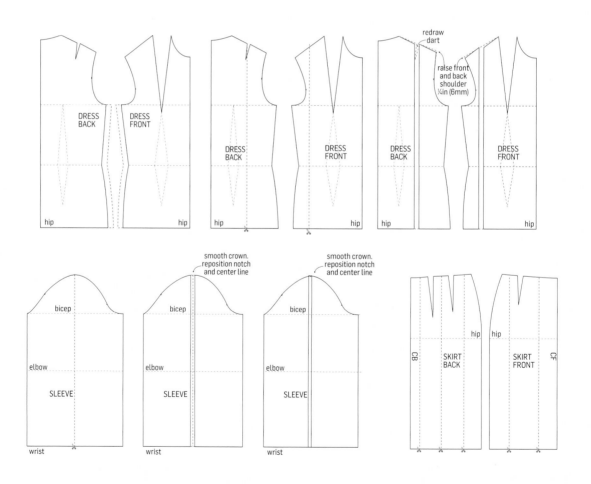

Shoulders

These adaptations will ensure that your garments sit correctly at the shoulder. **(1)** The shoulders and the crown of the sleeve will drop unsupported over narrow shoulders. **(2)** To correct this, slash the pattern as shown, and pivot the released section to remove width from the shoulder. Redraw the shoulderline and seam allowance.

(3) Wrinkles at the crown and shoulder indicate that the garment does not contain enough breadth for the shoulders. **(4)** To correct this, slash the pattern as shown and pivot the released section to give additional fullness over the shoulderline. Redraw and adjust seam allowance.

①

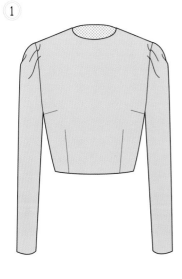

Dropping crown and shoulder

②

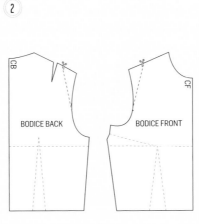

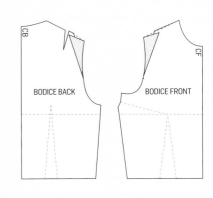

BODICE BACK   BODICE FRONT   BODICE BACK   BODICE FRONT

③

Wrinkled crown and shoulder

④

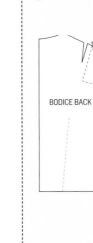
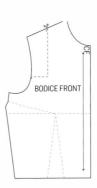
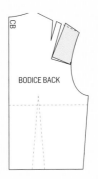
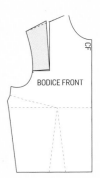

BODICE BACK   BODICE FRONT   BODICE BACK   BODICE FRONT

Sleeves

Poorly fitting sleeves will spoil the appearance of a garment and also be uncomfortable. **(1)** Diagonal folds at either the front or back armhole denote incorrectly distributed ease. This error is usually made in the construction phase, when ease is not correctly distributed during machining. To correct this, unpick the sleeve and smooth the excess ease either to the front or back of the sleevehead as required.

(2) An arm that is too large will cause your muslin to pull and feel uncomfortable to wear along most of its length. **(3)** To correct this, slash and spread the front and back of the sleeve to add more room for the ball of the shoulder. You may also need to add more height to the crown of the sleeve. The body will also need extra room in the armhole; pivot the released sections and

redraw the armhole and, if affected, the dart. Adjust the seam allowances. **(4)** Excess fabric will sag and wrinkle as it drops over too narrow an arm. **(5)** To correct this, cut the sleeve along its own length and overlap to the desired amount. Raise the armhole on both the front and the back body.

1

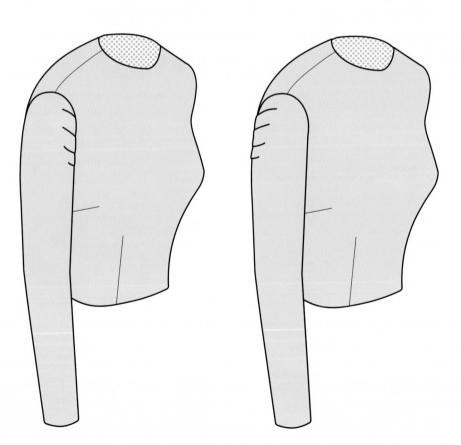

Incorrect ease

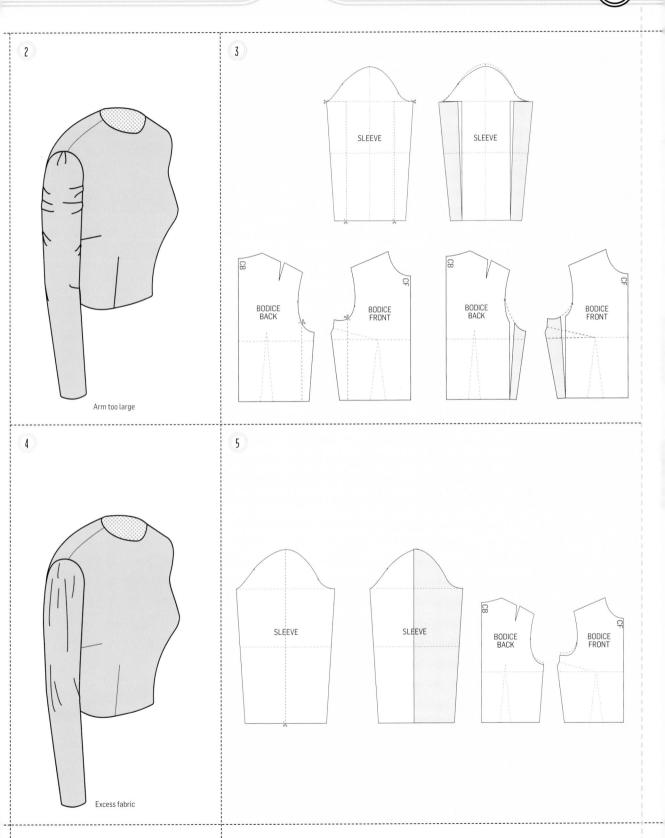

2

Arm too large

3

SLEEVE

SLEEVE

CB   BODICE BACK   BODICE FRONT   CF

CB   BODICE BACK   BODICE FRONT   CF

4

Excess fabric

5

SLEEVE

SLEEVE

CB   BODICE BACK   BODICE FRONT   CF

Bust

These adaptations will help to correct fitting problems in the bust area. **(1)** A small bust will cause your garment to collapse and crease over the bustline. **(2)** To correct this, cut your pattern into quarters through the center of the waist dart and the bustline. Overlap the pieces to the required amount. Redraw the shoulder seam and seam

allowances. You should also adjust any skirt pieces that are to be sewn to the waistline to accommodate the decreased waist measurement. **(3)** A large bust will cause your garment to strain across the bustline. **(4)** To correct this, cut your pattern piece into quarters through the center of the waist dart and the bustline. Spread the pieces to

the required amount and redraw the waist and bust darts, noting their increased width at the base of the dart legs. You should also adjust any skirt pieces that are to be sewn to the waistline to accommodate the increased waist measurement.

1

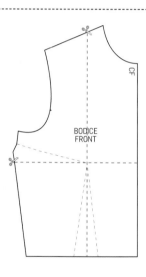

2

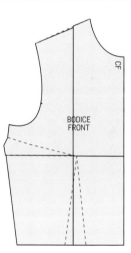

Small bust

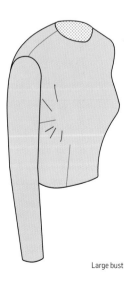

3

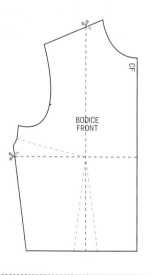

4

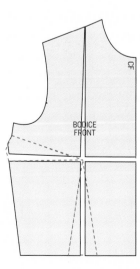

Large bust

Back

The adjustments below can resolve fitting problems across the back. **(1)** A narrow back will cause your garment to collapse over the shoulder blades. **(2)** To correct this, draw two lines, connecting each side of the shoulder dart to the base of the waist dart. If a shoulder dart is not present in your style, reduce the front shoulderline to match.

(3) A garment without enough space for a wide back will wrinkle over the shoulders. It will also pull at the armholes and, unless corrected, can cause a limited range of movement for the arms. **(4)** To correct this, cut the pattern piece as directed in the diagram, moving the released section to make more breadth across the upper back.

Redraw the side seam and shoulder dart, noting the wider shoulder dart position if applicable; if not, you may need to create one to reduce the difference in the back shoulderline compared with the front.

Narrow back

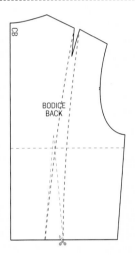
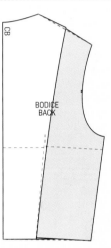

Wide back

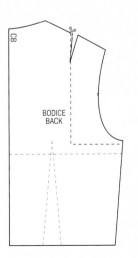
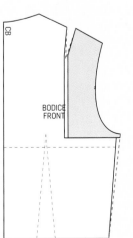

Laying out and cutting fabric

Taking care during the layout, cutting, and marking stages of garment construction ensures that you achieve the best possible fit and appearance, as well as the most economical use of fabric.

Grain

Woven fabrics are made up of warp and weft threads and this is what gives the fabric its grain. Strong warp threads run along the whole length of the fabric, making it least likely to stretch along its length. Weft threads are woven over and under the warp threads, backward and forward along its width, allowing the fabric a slight give in this direction. This "give" makes the weft grain particularly suitable for positioning across the body. The true bias of a fabric runs across the fabric at a 45-degree angle; as there are no threads running directly through this angle, the fabric is at its most stretchy. Bias-cut clothes mold and stretch to the body; lingerie, eveningwear, and many styles from the 1930s often feature bias cutting. When the fibers are woven, the edges of the fabric are given a firm finish to prevent fraying—this is called the selvage. The grain of a woven fabric affects the way a garment hangs and drapes; placing your pattern pieces "off grain," even in the interest of fabric economy, can twist and distort the finished garment, spoiling the appearance of the item.

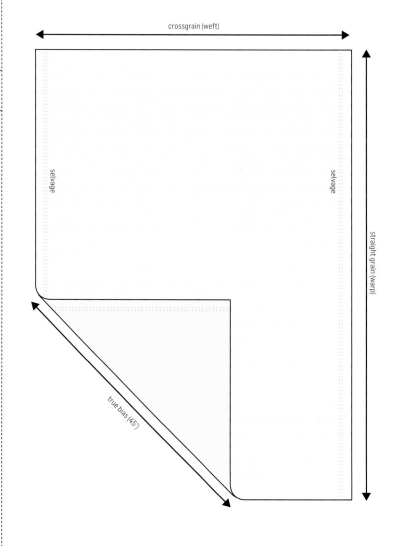

crossgrain (weft)

selvage

selvage

straight grain (warp)

true bias (45°)

Laying out

Before cutting out your pattern pieces, check that the grain of your fabric has not been distorted during milling processes such as printing, finishing, or rolling. To see if the fabric is "on grain," straighten each end of the fabric length; snip through the selvage and if possible draw a weft thread from the fabric and cut along the width of the fabric. Many fabrics tear easily along their width; after the preparatory selvage snip has been made, the fabric can be torn from selvage to selvage. Take care when using this method, however, as it can pull your fabric off grain. Lay your fabric on a flat surface, folding and pinning the fabric selvage to selvage. If the fabric lies flat, the grainlines will run at right angles to each other, which means the fabric is ready for use. To straighten fabric that is off grain, gently pull the fabric across its true bias, working along the length. Pressing with plenty of steam should ensure your fabric now lies true. When you lay your pattern pieces onto your fabric, use a tape measure or the pattern tool to check that they are aligned correctly with the grain before you cut them.

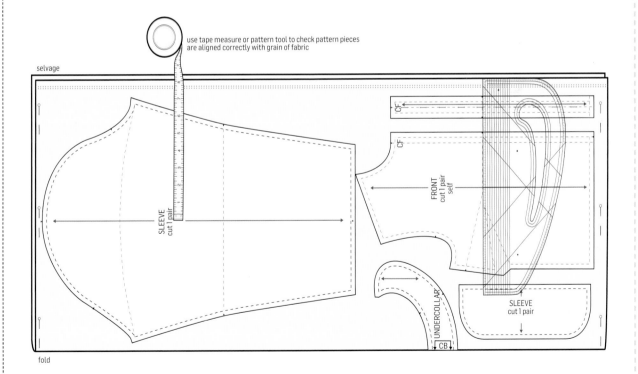

use tape measure or pattern tool to check pattern pieces are aligned correctly with grain of fabric

selvage

SLEEVE
cut 1 pair

FRONT
cut 1 pair
self

UNDERCOLLAR

CB

SLEEVE
cut 1 pair

fold

CHAPTER 9

Construction

This chapter outlines the fundamental stages in constructing a garment. Seams are a vital consideration, as they form the structure of a piece; choosing the appropriate seam will improve the garment's appearance and also how long it lasts, while hems are fundamental in achieving a professional finish. Adding zippers or a side opening are simple ways of adapting a garment; embellishments such as rouleaux loops and bows may be just what you need to realize the garment you desire.

Fishtail skirt.
Dollchops Clothing

Darts

Wedge darts

Wedge darts are denoted by notches in the seam allowance and a drill hole at the apex. The drill hole should be marked either with a tailor's tack or an alternative marking method. To sew a basic wedge dart, fold the fabric in half, with right sides together, bringing the notches together. Pin into position and stitch along the dart line toward the apex. As the point of the dart is reached, reduce the stitch length rather than backstitching, which can form an unsightly bubble. Tie off loose threads to finish.

Contour darts

Contour darts are diamond-shaped; they provide shaping from the bust through the waist and hips. Contour darts are marked with drill holes to denote their width and upper and lower reaches. To construct a contour dart, fold the fabric with right sides facing and sew from the center of the dart to the upper or lower apex, reducing stitch length as for a basic wedge dart. Repeat to complete the dart.

Dart tucks

A dart tuck is stitched only partway along the dart length marked on the pattern; it can be used in place of either a wedge or a contour dart. To convert a regular dart into a wedge dart, simply mark new drill holes part of the way along the dart line on the pattern and transfer only these to the fabric, ignoring the original drill hole marked at the apex. Fold the fabric in half with right sides facing to match drill holes and sew using the new markings as a guide, backstitching at the end to secure. Lightly press the finished dart tuck. You can either press the dart excess to one side, or you can flatten and divide the fullness equally on either side of the stitch line.

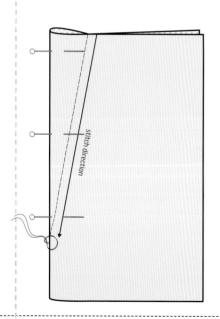

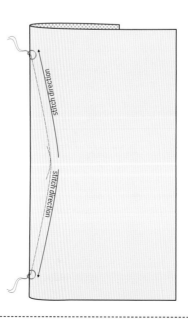

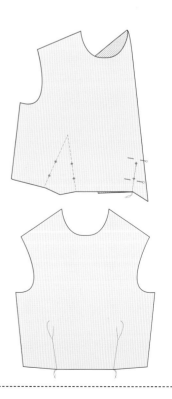

Gathers

A pattern will usually use notches to denote a gathered section; these may match a smaller measurement and notches on an adjacent pattern piece. **(1)** Set the machine to the longest stitch and make two lines of machine basting either side of the sew line. Leave the loose thread ends long and do not backstitch at either end of the stitch line. The gathering stitches should extend a short way beyond the notch markings to ensure the gathering is extended evenly from notch to notch. If you fail to do this, your gathered section will flatten prematurely. Pull the thread ends on the bobbin thread to draw the fabric into gathers, sliding the fabric along and distributing fabric evenly between notches. **(2)** Return the stitch setting to the usual stitch length and, with right sides facing, match notches and pin into position. **(3)** Stitch to the adjacent panel and remove the gathering stitches.

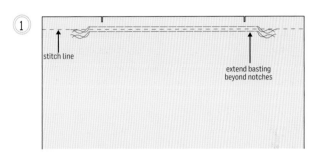

stitch line

extend basting beyond notches

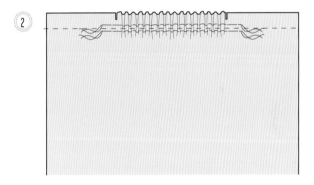

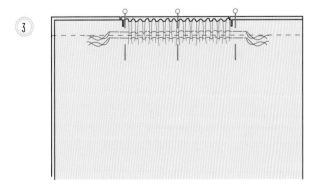

SEWING TIP

You need to remove gathering stitches once the garment sections are constructed; sewing with a contrasting thread can help the basting stitches to stand out more clearly against your fabric. Changing only the bobbin thread rather than the top thread will speed up this process.

Sleeves: tubular method

(1) Set your sewing machine to its largest stitch and sew two rows of machine basting between the notches and within the seam allowance. **(2)** Use basting stitch to gauge the ease in the crown of the sleeve. Ensure that fullness is distributed evenly and note how the cap begins to form at the shoulder. Sew the underarm seam, then press the seam allowance open and turn to the right side. **(3)** Sew the darts, the side seam, and the shoulder seam, then press the seam allowances open. Turn the bodice to the wrong side and insert the tubed sleeve into the armhole. Note that the sleeve and the bodice are placed right sides together. Match the notches and seams, pinning the sleeve at these points first. Place more pins evenly around the sleeve and hand-baste the sleeve in place, removing the pins as you work. Turn the bodice to the right side to check the fit and balance. Once you are satisfied with the sleeve placement, turn the bodice back to the wrong side and sew it into position. Ensure that all seam allowances are laying flat in the correct position as you sew.

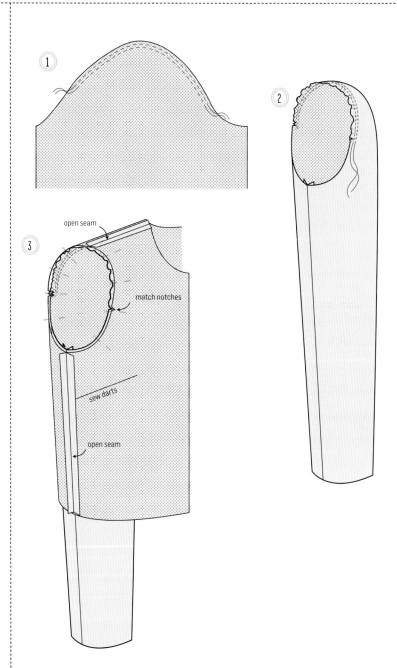

1

2

open seam

3

match notches

sew darts

open seam

Seams

Preparation

(1) Pin seams prior to construction to ensure that garment pieces are lined up accurately. Pin pieces together at either end first, then at notch markings. You can then distribute pins along the length of the piece at 3 to 4-inch (7.5 to 10cm) intervals. Avoid putting in too many pins, as this will make the pieces difficult to handle on the machine. Place pins horizontally across the sewing line and remove each pin before it is drawn under the machine foot. Try not to sew over pins, as this can result in a broken or irregular stitch line.

(2) Use basting or tacking stitches to temporarily secure parts of a garment, ready for machine stitching. You can make these stitches by hand, with a large running stitch, or by selecting the largest stitch on your machine. It is not necessary to baste all seams during construction, as pinning is often enough, but tricky areas such as a zipper or a sleeve will benefit from this process.

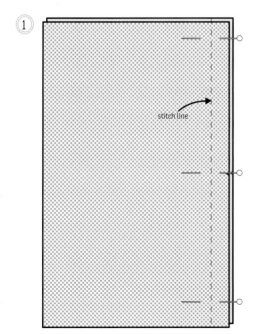

stitch line

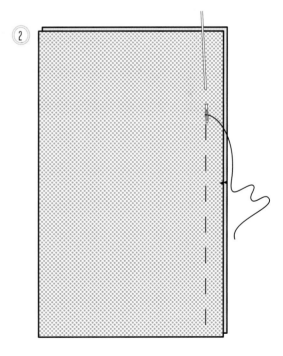

Types of seam

PLAIN

A plain seam is the seam most commonly used for the garments in this book. **(1)** Place the right sides of the fabric together and sew a single line of stitch on the stitch line, usually ¼–½in (6mm–1.2cm) from the edge. **(2)** You can splay and press the seam allowances to give an open seam. This technique is mainly used on style lines and side seams to give a flat look from the right side of the garment. **(3)** Alternatively, you can press the seam allowances to one side, giving a closed seam. These are commonly used at waistbands and facing edges. **(4)** The completed seam from the right side.

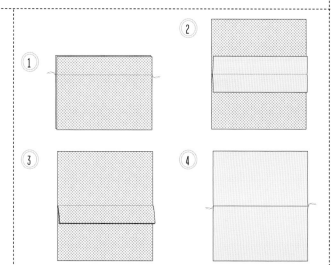

FRENCH

This self-neatening seam is often used on sheer fabrics. It is also suitable for garments that receive heavy wear and laundering, such as lingerie. The French knickers (page 118) use this seam. **(1)** With ½in (1.2cm) seam allowances, place the sections wrong sides together with the stitch lines matching. Stitch a seam ¼in (6mm) in from the seam edge and trim back to ⅛in (3mm). **(2)** Press the seam allowances open and fold the seam right sides together. **(3)** Stitch another line ¼in (6mm) in from the edge. Open the finished seam and press to one side.

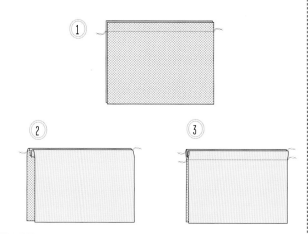

WELT

A welt seam is suitable for medium- to heavyweight fabrics. It uses two pieces with different seam allowances, one with ¼in (6mm) and the other with ½in (1.2cm). If you are using a pattern that is not already prepared for sewing, trim down the seam allowance after cutting the fabric. If you are using a fabric that is liable to fray, you must neaten the longer seam allowance before you sew it. **(1)** Neaten the edge and place the pieces right sides together with the stitch lines matching, then sew down the stitch line. **(2)** Press the seam, folding the overlocked edge over to cover the shorter raw edge. Turn the fabric to the right side and topstitch it so the longer seam allowance is caught on the underside and the raw edge is enclosed. **(3)** The finished result gives a distinctive raised appearance.

neaten edge if necessary

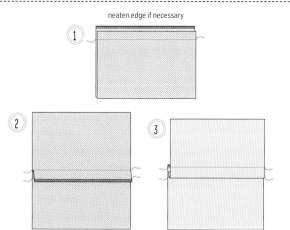

PIPED

This decorative seam can be used to enhance style lines. It can be used with many fabrics, but thinner to medium-weight materials are best used for the piping casing, as thicker fabrics may be too bulky. Consider using a piped seam around the edge of a Peter Pan collar or a patch pocket. For an alternative look, you can remove the piping once you have stitched the seam. You can use store-bought binding as a piping casing, or make one from your own fabrics following these steps. **(1)** Cut a bias strip of fabric for the binding 1½in (4cm) wide for the length needed. You might need to join strips together to achieve the desired length. **(2)** Fold the bias strips in half, wrong sides together, enclosing a length of piping against the folded edge. **(3)** With the zipper foot attached, sew a line of stitching close to the piping. **(4)** Matching the seam edges, sew the piping right sides together to one of the garment sections with the zipper foot along the same line. **(5)** Attach the other garment section as before and press the seams outward. **(6)** The piped seam from the right side. **(7)** The seam from the wrong side.

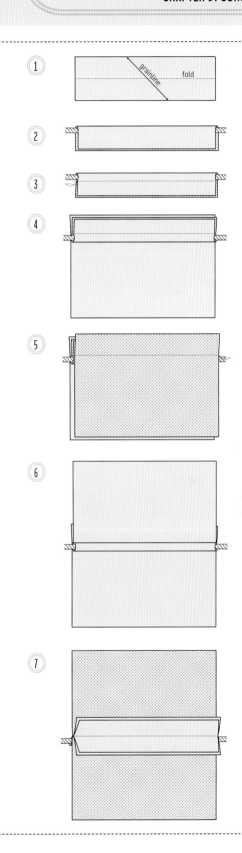

Finishing techniques

NEATENING

Depending on your fabric, you may need to neaten the edges of a garment that is not faced or lined to reduce fraying during construction and wear. Serged (overlocked) seams are evident in manufactured apparel from the 1950s, and became standard from the 1960s onward. If you don't have access to this machinery, overstitching or zigzag settings can be found on most modern sewing machines.

STAYSTITCHING

Staystitching is a permanent line of stitch made ½in (1.2cm) from the cut edge of a garment section prior to joining. It helps prevent the piece from stretching and distorting, especially in curved areas such as the neckline or armhole.

TOPSTITCHING

Topstitching is a line of stitching made at varying distances from the edge of a seam. It strengthens the seam and keeps areas such as facings in place. Topstitching is usually made using a longer stitch length and a thicker thread than that used for the seam. You can use a contrasting thread or decorative stitch if desired. You can sew topstitching on both sides of a seam or on one side only. It can be particularly effective around the edge of a pocket or a collar.

SINK-STITCHING

Sink-stitching is a nearly invisible line of stitching that is sunk into the ditch of a completed seam or turned-out section of a garment, such as the collar or cuff on a blouse or a skirt waistband.

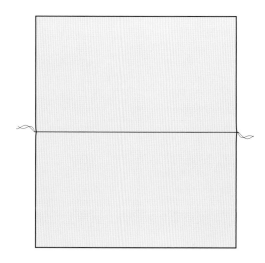

MITERING CORNERS

As parts of your garment are sewn to one another, it is often necessary to miter seam-allowance corners to reduce bulk. **(1)** Stitch the garment sections together. **(2)** Trim the seam allowance at a 45-degree angle.

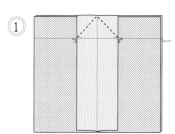

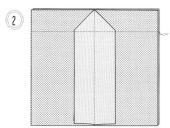

EDGESTITCHING

Edgestitching is a line of topstitching made close to the edge of a seam. It is both decorative and functional, strengthening the seam and keeping areas such as facings in place. Edgestitching, like topstitching, is usually made in a longer stitch length than that of the seam and can be worked on **(1)** an open or **(2)** a closed seam.

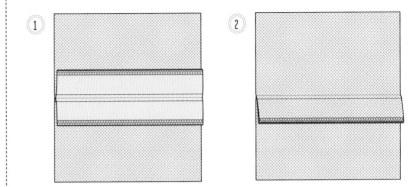

UNDERSTITCHING

Understitching is a single row of edgestitch. It is used to prevent profile edges, such as the neckline, armhole facing, or lining, from rolling outward. When made correctly, it is not visible from the right side of the garment, unlike a top- or edgestitch. **(1)** Once you have sewn the seam attaching the garment inner, lightly press both seam allowances inward toward the facing/lining, then sew the understitch row from the right side of the garment, through both layers of the seam allowance and facing. **(2)** This catches the seam allowances to the facing, stabilizing the seam and ensuring that the facing is not seen from the right side of the garment.

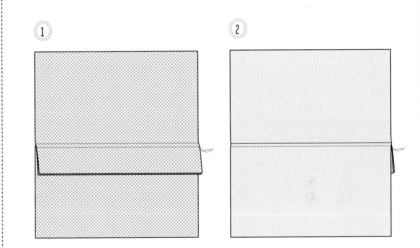

TRIMMING

Seams can be trimmed back to ⅜₆in (4mm), or graded by trimming back allowances to different widths, say ³⁄₁₆ and ⁵⁄₁₆in (4 and 7mm). This removes bulk and allows seams to lay flatter. Grading ensures that seam allowances don't leave a visible ridge from the right side. If you are using a combination of grading and understitching, make sure you complete the understitching process first.

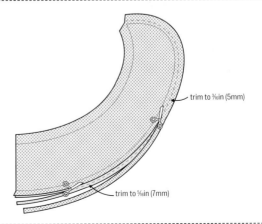

trim to ³⁄₁₆in (5mm)

trim to ⁵⁄₁₆in (7mm)

Binding seams

HOMEMADE BINDING

Binding is a versatile method of finishing
that encloses the raw fabric edge with
a strip of bias-cut fabric. You can buy
ready-prepared binding, or make it from
your own fabric. **(1)** Cut 1½in (4cm) strips at
a 45-degree angle to the grain. **(2)** If required,
join strips to achieve the necessary length.

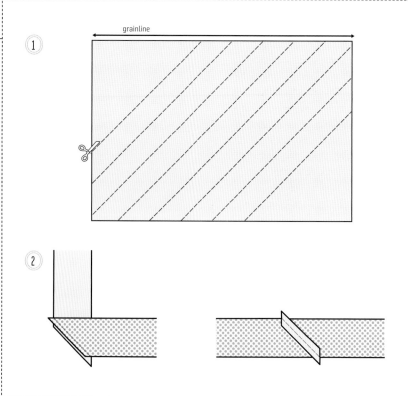

BOUND SEAM

You can use binding to neaten the seams in
an unlined garment or to finish or decorate
profile edges such as necklines, armholes,
collars, and hems. Consider a contrasting
color or fabric for effect. **(1)** Cut a bias strip
of fabric for the binding 1½in (4cm) wide.
Press this strip into four equal sections
along its length, or use a bias tape folder
if available. **(2)** Sew the strip onto one of the
garment sections, right sides together along
the pressed crease line. **(3)** Fold the binding
strip, then fold again onto the wrong side so
that it encloses the raw edge, and press.
From the right side, edgestitch or sink-stitch
the folded edge on the wrong side. Repeat
for the other side. Sew the sections together
as for a plain seam.

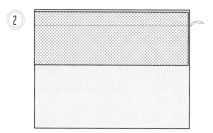

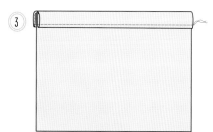

BOUND FACING

A bound facing uses a bias strip of fabric to neaten profile edges such as necklines, armholes, or hems; it does not show on the right side of the garment. A bound facing can be completed with a machine edgestitch, or used in combination with a handstitch, as shown here. **(1)** Place the right side of the binding to the right side of the garment, turning back a short section at the start of the bias strip to give a clean finish. This turn-back should straddle the seam allowances to reduce bulk. **(2)** Sew into position. Note that the end of the bias strip does not require a turn-back. **(3)** Turn the garment inside out and fold the bias strip over to conceal the raw edges. Turn the raw edge of the bias strip under and stitch it into position.

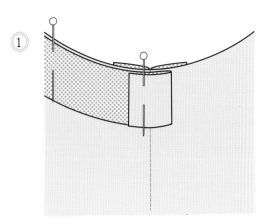

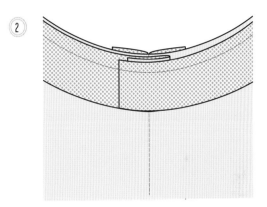

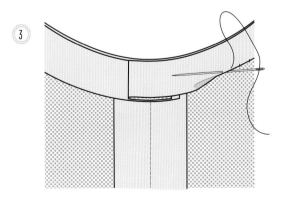

Hems

Single turn

This is suitable for a wide variety of fabrics.
(1) If necessary, neaten the edge of the
fabric. (2) Fold over the hem allowance
and stitch to secure.

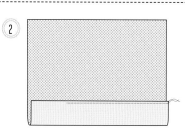

Hemming stitch

This handstitched finish can be completed
with a single- or a double-turned hem.
Working from right to left, bring the needle
up through the hem edge. Directly opposite
and fractionally above the hem, take a stitch,
ensuring you catch only one or two threads
of the fabric, then move the needle diagonally
through the hem edge. Repeat for the length
of the hem, spacing each stitch roughly
¼–⅜in (6–10mm) apart; do not draw the
thread tight, as this creates a tension that
may cause stitch work to show from the
right side.

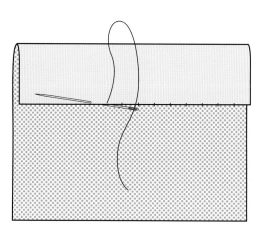

Double turn

This self-neatening hem is suitable for
non-bulky fabrics and can be sewn in
conjunction with a topstitched or a handstitched finish. You can adjust the hem turn
allowance as the individual design dictates.
(1) Fold the first turn allowance up. (2) Fold
the second turn allowance and topstitch.
The raw edge is concealed in the double-
turned fabric.

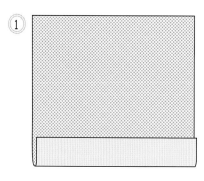

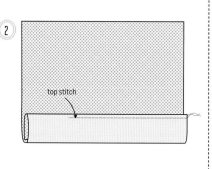

top stitch

Machine-rolled

(1) Select a suitable size stitch in relation to your fabric and sew ⅛in (3mm) from the fabric edge. **(2)** Roll the fabric against the first line of stitching to create a very narrow hem, then sew a second line of stitching. **(3)** Roll the fabric against the second line of stitching and complete the hem with a third line of stitching.

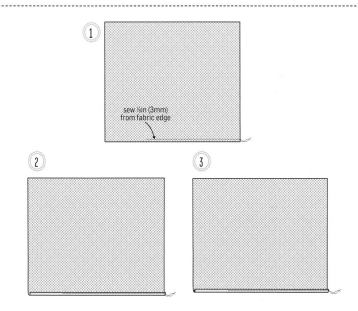

sew ⅛in (3mm)
from fabric edge

Hand-rolled

(1) Machine stitch approximately ¼in (6mm) from the edge and trim close to the stitch line. **(2)** Fold the fabric to the wrong side about ⅛in (3mm) from the stitch line and press the crease into position. **(3)** With a matching thread, take a small stitch through the fold, ensuring you catch only a single thread of the fabric. Make another stitch at an angle just above the raw edge, pulling the thread to roll the hem every few stitches.

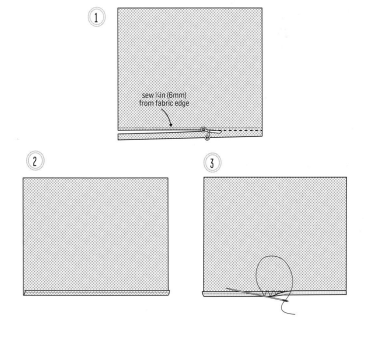

sew ¼in (6mm)
from fabric edge

Side openings

Zipper closures, or side openings, became available at the turn of the twentieth century, but were not regularly used in ready-to-wear clothing until the 1930s. Many dressmaker-made clothes and closings relied on a side opening with a press-stud fastening up until the 1950s. Although most of the garments in this book utilize a zipper opening, these can easily be converted into a side opening using the following method.

The following instructions describe the process for insertion in a dress side seam that is closed at both ends, but this method can easily be adapted for an open-end fastening in a waisted garment such as a bodice, skirt, or pants. If you are using a seam-neatening method such as overlocking or a zigzag stitch, you will need to neaten the edges of both plackets prior to construction.

(1) First draft the placket facings. Draft the front placket to the length of the opening plus twice the seam allowance. Draft the back placket to the length of the opening plus four times the seam allowance. Add seam allowances to the top and bottom of front and back plackets only.
(2) Prepare the garment side seam. Press seam allowances open at the side seam; the waist seam should be positioned as per specific garment construction instructions. (3) With right sides facing, lay the front placket to the side seam and machine through the seam allowance only, stitching close to the fold. (4) Grade the seam allowance on the front placket only to reduce bulk. (5) Fold the placket into position.
(6) Lay the back placket, with right sides facing, and machine through the seam allowances only close to the folded edge. (7) Grade the back placket seam allowances only. (8) Fold the placket into position and stitch through the seam allowances and placket only to secure the placket. (9) Stitch horizontally through all layers bar the garment to secure the plackets. (10) Finally, sew press studs to the front and back plackets. A hook and eye can be used at the center of the waist to avoid press studs popping open during wear.

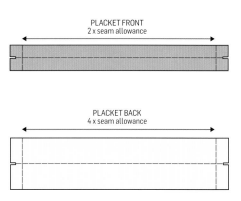

PLACKET FRONT
2 x seam allowance

PLACKET BACK
4 x seam allowance

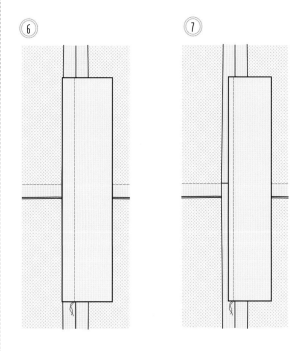

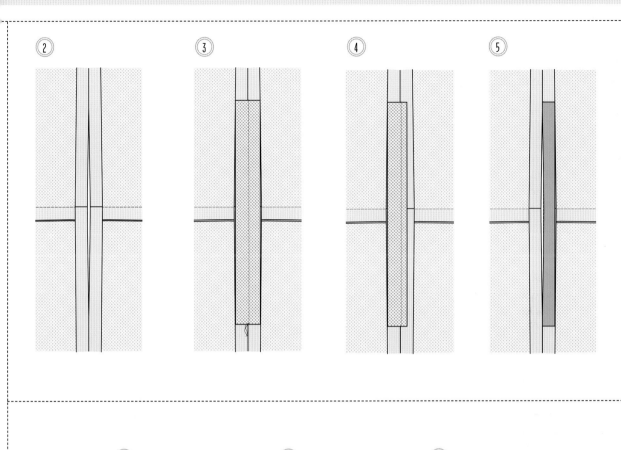

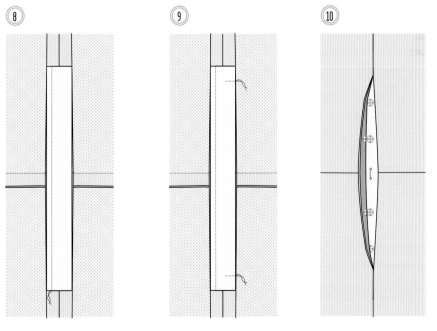

Pockets

Patch pocket

(1) Plan the pocket and the turnback. Mark the position of the pocket on the garment with tailor tacks. (2) Grow the turnback onto the patch pocket, add seam allowances, and mark the fold line with a notch. (3) Press the seam allowances to the wrong side and miter the corners. (4) Sew the turnback hem. Lightly press the turnback. (5) Sew the pocket to the main garment, using backstitching or a more decorative stitch to reinforce the pocket opening.

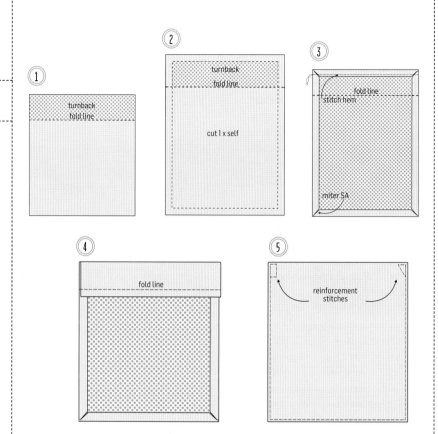

Curved patch pocket

(1) Plan the pocket as for the patch pocket above. Fold and neaten the pocket facing. (2) Loosen the upper tension on your machine and sew around the curve, leaving long threads to gauge the curve in the next step. Pull the bobbin thread tight, encouraging the seam allowance to turn. (3) Use a cardboard copy of the pocket as a pressing template and flatten the seam allowance. Return the tension to your usual setting and continue construction as for the patch pocket.

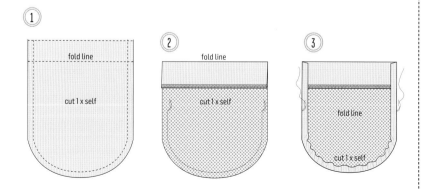

Welt pocket

(1) Plan welt size and position. Draft the welt pattern piece at twice the width of finished welt × finished welt length. Add a ⅝in (1.5cm) seam allowance all around. Draft the welt facing pattern to 1 × finished welt width and add ⅝in (1.5cm) to its length. Add a ⅝in (1.5cm) seam allowance all around). (2) Plan the pocket bag depth. Draft the pocket bag to those measurements, add a ⅝in (1.5cm) seam allowance and cut 2 × lining.
(3) Interface WS of fabric and mark the welt opening with drill holes. Note that the innermost drill hole is ⅝in (1.5cm) from the outer edge markings. (4) Lay the welt and the welt facing on the main fabric with wrong sides together and sew in line with the drill holes. (5) Turn the work over to WS and cut the pocket opening on the garment only, then miter the corners. (6) Fold along stitch line and post welts through pocket opening. Fold mitered triangles to WS.
(7) Fold the welt facing upward temporarily and fold welt downward, ready to attach the pocket bags. (8) With right sides together, sew one pocket bag to the welt, as shown in the diagram. (9) Fold the welt in half and drop the pocket bag into position, noting that the seam allowance is facing toward the garment. Press the seam allowance open. (10) With RS together, sew the second pocket bag to the welt facing. (11) Drop the welt facing into position and press the seam allowance open. Sew the pocket bags as for the welt and, if required, neaten the pocket bag as one.

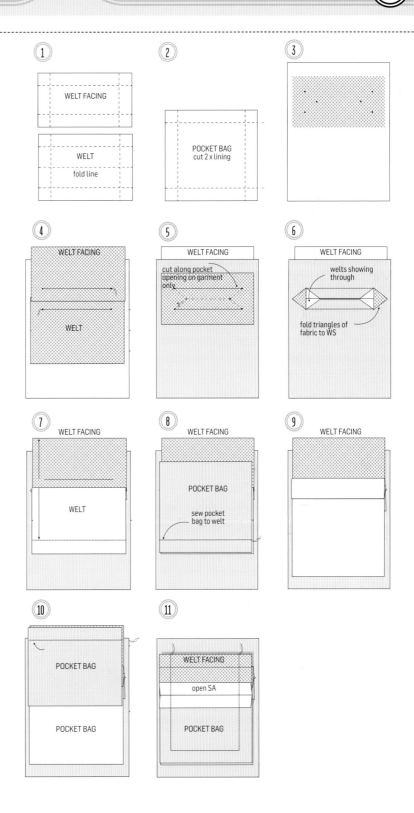

Zippers

Concealed

(1) Machine-stitch the side seam, using a longer basting stitch for the section of the seam where the zipper will be inserted. Turn the garment to the wrong side and press the seam open. (2) Lay the zipper with the right side down over the seam, with the teeth or coil centralized over the seam and the pull tab upward. The pull tab should be positioned ¼in (6mm) below the sew line and the bottom stop approximately ⅛in (3mm) above the lower end of the opening. Pin, then hand-tack the zipper into position. (3) Turn the garment over to the right side and, using the zipper foot, machine-stitch in position, approximately ¼in (6mm) either side of the seam. Pivot at the corners with the needle down, and complete an equal number of stitches either side of the seam. Trim the zipper tape in line with the edge of the garment and remove the machine- and hand-tacking.

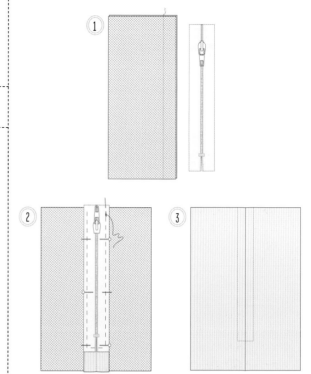

Semi-concealed

(1) Machine-stitch the side seam, using a longer basting stitch for the section of the seam where the zipper will be inserted, and backstitch at the bottom of the opening. (2) Turn the garment to the wrong side and press the seam open. (3) Fold back the right-hand side (if placing on a center back seam), or the back section (if placing on a side seam) of the garment. (4) Fold the seam allowance under ⅛in (3mm) from the tacked seam. (5) Place the folded edge of the seam allowance against the right side of the zipper tape, butted up against the teeth or coil. Hand-tack into position, then, with the zipper foot in place and the needle set to the left-hand side of the zipper foot, machine-stitch from the bottom of the zipper toward the top. (6) Turn the garment to the right side, allowing the unstitched side of the garment to lay flat on top of the zipper, and baste into position. With the needle set to the right side of the zipper foot, machine through all layers, first along the bottom edge, then up the length of the zipper approximately ½in (1.2mm) from the tacked seam.

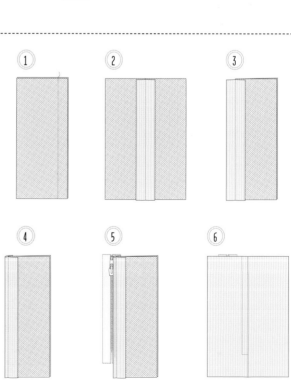

Rouleaux loops

For straps

Rouleaux loops can be constructed in a variety of widths to create a strap or decorative element for a garment. They are cut on the bias grain to facilitate ease of turning, which is more relevant the thinner the strap is. The cutting method for bias strips is described on page 168.

PLAIN

(1) First prepare the bias strip. Make the length required, joining bias strips if necessary, 2 x width of the finished strip plus ⅜in (1cm) seam allowance. **(2)** Fold the bias strip horizontally with right sides facing.
(3) Sew the strip ⅜in (1cm) from the edge, widening at one edge, thus creating a funnel to begin turning the loop through. Leave threads long to facilitate turning. **(4)** Trim the seam allowance close to the line of stitching.
(5) Thread the loose ends through a darning needle and knot the ends. **(6)** Pass the needle through the channel eye first to avoid snagging on fabric. **(7)** Carefully turn the loop to the right side.

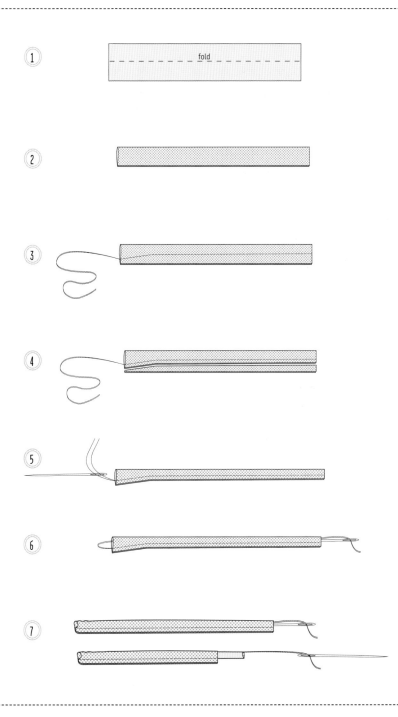

CORDED ROULEAUX LOOP

A corded rouleaux loop gives more structure than a plain one. This can be particularly useful when using loops as an opening or decorative feature on a garment. **(1)** First, prepare the bias strip as described for the plain loop and cut a piece of piping cord approximately twice the finished length. Fold the bias strip with right sides facing and place the piping against the fold. **(2)** Use a zipper foot to machine close to the piping cord. **(3)** Ensure the cord is not caught during sewing and, again, widen the stitching at one edge to facilitate turning. Sew through all layers to secure the cord to the bias strip. **(4)** Use the cord to turn the loop to the right side.

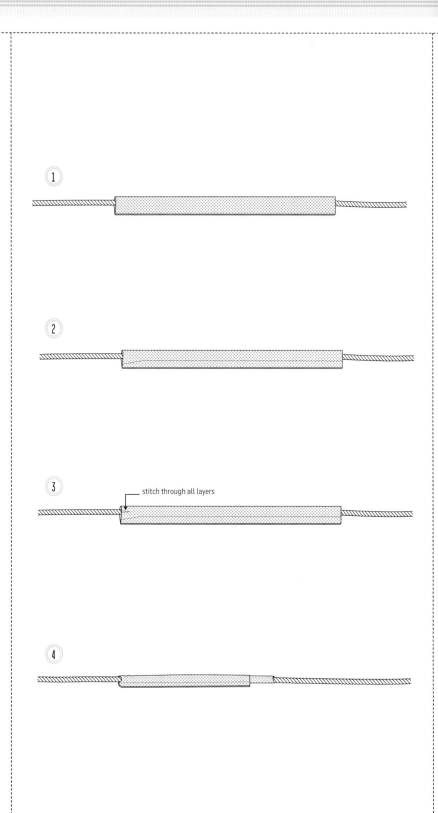

1

2

3

stitch through all layers

4

For button closures

Rouleaux loops can also be used to create a loop for a button closure; this is particularly suitable for edge-to-edge openings such as a waistband. You could use this method as an alternative for the hook-and-eye opening on the bustier and petticoat (page 124) or the cuff of the mini dress (page 30). Consider using self-covered buttons for a truly bespoke finish. A plain or corded rouleaux loop can be used as the design dictates.

SINGLE LOOP OPENING

(1) First plan and prepare the loops. If using plain rouleaux loops, flatten the edge as shown and pin to opening with the folded edge facing away from the seam allowance. Stitch the loops into position with two rows of machine stitching. (2) Lay facing or lining with right sides facing on top of the rouleaux, thus sandwiching the loops between garment pieces. (3) Sew as the design dictates. Turn the garment to the right side and lightly press.

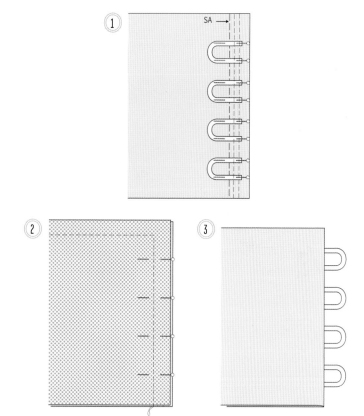

CONTINUOUS LOOP OPENING

If the planned rouleaux loops are close together, it is advisable to use a continuous line of loops to make positioning and sewing more uniform. (1) Plan and prepare the loops and stitch the loops with two lines of machine stitching. (2) Snip each loop within seam allowances to ensure the loop lays flat and bulk is reduced. (3) Turn the garment to the right side.

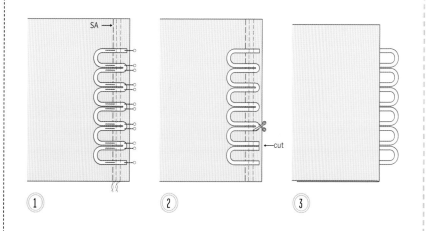

Bows

Single bow

In the following example we make a five-inch (12.5cm) bow, but this method can be used to create a bow of just about any size. You can create a bow on the straight or on the bias grain. **(1)** Prepare the bow pattern as the design dictates. Decide on the finished width and length of the bow and create a paper template. Add seam allowances ¼in (6mm) all around. **(2)** Prepare the bow center using the previous measurements as a guide. Add ¼in (6mm) seam allowances all around. **(3)** Fold the bow in half, with right sides facing, and sew the open edge, leaving a gap for bagging out. **(4)** Miter the corners to reduce bulk and turn to the right side. Press. Depending on the size of your finished bow, you may be able to bag out the center using the method described above. Cutting on the bias will enable bagging out of smaller shapes, but if this is not possible, simply press the seam allowances to the wrong side as shown and fold in half. **(5)** Fold the bow in half and sew, using the measurements set out in step 1 as a guide. **(6)** Open the bow out. **(7)** Fold and sew the center section around the bow.

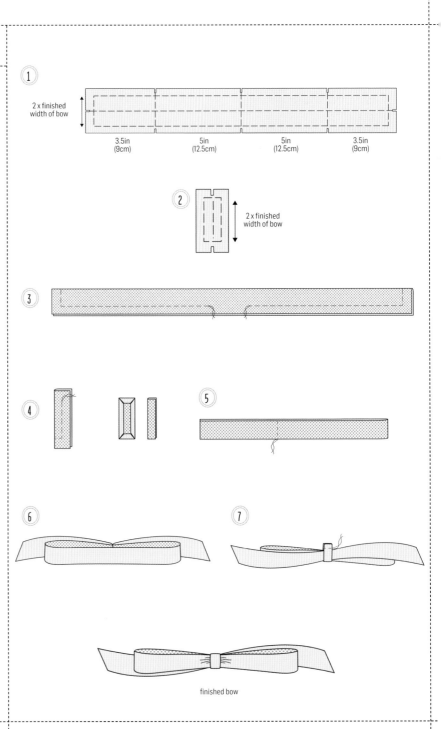

finished bow

Double bow

To make a double-stacked bow, follow the same method as for a single bow. You can use a bagged-out section (as described for the single bow, opposite) or a piece of braid or ribbon, as described below. **(1)** First plan the bow. **(2)** Plan the center section at twice the width of the bow plus seam allowances at upper and lower edge for joining. **(3)** Using the measurements from step 1 as a guide, stitch the bow section. **(4)** Open the bow out. **(5)** Sew the center section around the bow.

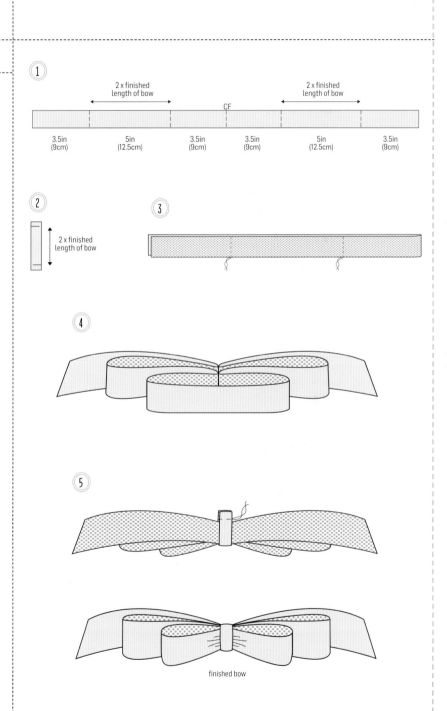

finished bow

Scallops

Scalloped hem

You can easily convert the hem on an existing garment into a more decorative scalloped hem. These instructions describe the technique for converting the A-line skirt of the maxi dress on page 36, but you can also apply this method to a sleeve hem, jacket front, or pocket flap. **(1)** Prepare the pattern, marking on the desired scallop shape within the seam allowances. Draw in the upper edge of the facing. Copy the patterns, adding ¼in (6mm) seam allowances to the scallop edges and upper facing edge and ½in (1.2cm) to the side seams. **(2)** Construct the skirt as usual. With right sides together, sew the facing side seams. Press the seam allowances open and hem the upper facing edge. **(3)** Turn the garment to the right side, and with right sides together sew the facing along the scalloped edge. Miter the center of each scallop to reduce bulk and aid turning. Turn and press the facing into position, catching the facing seam allowances to the skirt seam allowance with a few hand-stitches or blind stitching all around.

1

facing line

2

3

Shell gathering

Shell gathering produces a gathered scallop edging that you can use to great effect to trim garments. You can make it from light-weight ribbon and braiding or from a folded strip of bias tape. **(1)** To construct shell gathering from bias strips, first cut a bias strip twice the desired finished width and approximately three times the finished length required. You may need to join several bias strips together to achieve the desired length (see page 168). **(2)** Fold the raw edges to meet each other in the center and press. **(3)** Set the machine to its longest stitch and sew a continuous zigzag along the length of your bias strip. You can experiment with other stitch patterns such as a scallop. **(4)** Draw the gathering stitch and distribute fullness along the length. Fasten off the threads securely. **(5)** Hand-sew the gathers to the garment as the design dictates. Here, we used alternating rows of wide and narrow shell gathering to decorate the hem of a circular skirt.

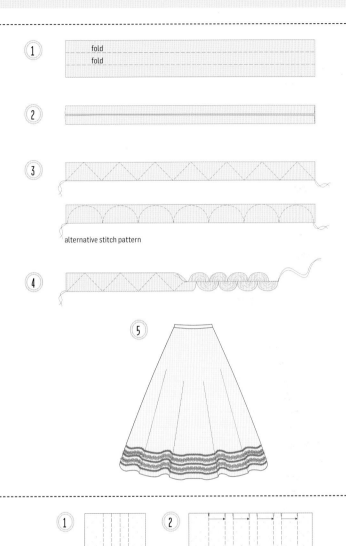

Shell tucks

Shell tucks create a scalloped finish to a regular pin tuck, such as those on the yoke of the 1960s mini dress (page 30). If the pattern piece does not have tucks, you can add them using the following method. **(1)** Mark tucks on the pattern with a dashed line, then cut each line to a separate pattern piece. **(2)** Add twice the finished tuck width between each pattern piece and add notches. **(3)** Sew the pin tucks and construct the garment as the design dictates. **(4)** Hand-sew each tuck with three overcast stitches to constrain the pin tuck, tie off securely, and repeat.

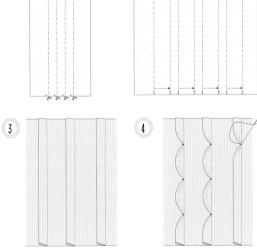

Contributors

Style overview entries

JO-ANN FORTUNE

(editor of www.vintagebrighton.com)

The little black dress, page 14

The Peter Pan collar, page 46

The printed scarf, page 132

SOPHIE O'KELLY

(www.sophieokelly.com

sophie.okelly@live.com)

Bias cutting, page 16

The natural waist, page 20

Buttons, page 44

The rever collar, page 48

The dog-eared collar, page 50

Shirt cuffs, page 52

Sports and leisurewear, page 76

Denim, page 80

The utility coat, page 88

The utility jacket, page 90

The utility skirt, page 92

The kimono jacket, page 94

The petticoat, page 112

The turban, page 134

DIANE LEYMAN

(www.notestoafurtherexcuse.com

diane@notestoafurtherexcuse.com)

The flapper dress, page 12

The pencil skirt, page 60

The circle skirt, page 62

The pleated skirt, page 64

The pillbox hat, page 136

GEMMA SEAGER

(www.mschickmedia.com

hello@retrochick.co.uk)

The halterneck, page 18

The playsuit, page 78

Support garments, page 110

Gloves, page 130

Images

ANN-MARIE FAULKNER MILLINERY

(annmariefaulkner.co.uk

hello@annmariefaulkner.co.uk)

Micro pom-pom fez, page 128

Silver glass pillbox, page 136

AUDREY ROGERS

(www.befrassy.com; www.frassyrags.com

audreyrogers@live.com;

dazed2dazzled@hotmail.com)

Pleated maxi skirt, page 64

Pleated mini skirt, page 65

CARRIE HARWOOD

(http://wishwishwish.net)

Numph top, page 4

Dress and cardigan, page 5

Shirt dress, page 10

Black dress with ruffle trims, page 15

Chiffon dress, page 20

Cardigan, page 44

Dress, page 45

Dog-eared collar, page 51

Shirt dress, page 46

Striped shirt, page 48

Dress shirt, page 53

Bootleg jeans, page 81

Yellow coat, page 86

COLETTE PATTERNS

(www.colettepatterns.com

service@colettepatterns.com)

Nutmeg petticoat, page 112

Cinammon petticoat, page 113

COMMERCIAL PATTERN ARCHIVE, SPECIAL COLLECTIONS, UNIVERSITY OF RHODE ISLAND LIBRARY

(uri.edu/library/special_collections/COPA)

Timeline images

1920s, page 8
(Archive no. 1927.334.BWS)

1930s, page 8
(Archive no. 1936.24.JSE)

1940s, page 8
(Archive no. 1944.193.BWS)

1950s, page 9
(Archive no. 1955.125.BWS)

1960s, page 9
(Archive no. 1967.6.JSE)

1970s, page 9
(Archive no. 1977.11.JSE)

Vintage pattern images

The flapper dress, page 12
(Archive no. 1927.29.URI)

The little black dress, page 4
(Archive no. 1962.51.JSE)

Bias cutting, page 16
(Archive no. 1933.4ab.JSE)

The halterneck, page 18
Archive no. 1952.51.URI)

The natural waist, page 20
(Archive no. 1951.421.BWS)

Buttons, page 44
(Archive no. 1956.120.BWS)

The Peter Pan collar, page 46
(Archive no. 1958.177.URI)

The rever collar, page 48
Archive no. 1946.183.BWS)

The dog-eared collar, page 50
(Archive no. 1971.11.JSE)

Shirt cuffs, page 52
(Archive no. 1977.79.URI)

The pencil skirt, page 60
(Archive no. 1957.135.URI)

The circle skirt, page 62
(Archive no. 1956.16.JSE)

The pleated skirt, page 64
(Archive no. 1943.103.URI)

Sports and leisurewear , page 76
(Archive no. 1940.142.BWS)

The playsuit, page 78
(Archive no. 1956.8.JSE)

Denim, page 80
(Archive no. 1973.125.URI)

The utility coat, page 88
(Archive no. 1944.19.URI)

The utility jacket, page 90
(Archive no. 1958.46.URI)

The utility skirt, page 92
(Archive no. 1942.204.BWS)

The kimono jacket, page 94
(Archive no. 1936.149.BWS)

Support garments, page 110
(Archive no. 1935.15.BWS)

Petticoats and slips, page 112
(Archive no. 1942.11.JSE)

Gloves, page 130
(Archive no. 1948.101.URI)

The printed scarf, page 132
(Archive no. 1945.44.JSE)

The turban, page 134
(Archive no. 1940.9.JSE)

The pillbox hat, page 136
(Archive no. 1952.24.URI)

DECADES OF STYLE PATTERN COMPANY
(www.decadesofstyle.com
info@decadesofstyle.com)
Button dress, page 45
(photography: Christina McFall)
Tulip kimono, page 94
(photography: Christina McFall)

EXILE VINTAGE
(shopexile.etsy.com)
Dog-eared collar dress, page 50
Apple print dog-eared collar dress,
page 50

JACQUELINE ROSE
(www.FashionSnag.com)
Knitted halterneck, page 18

LISA MARSHALL
(shoesandsashimiblogspot.com)
Chic turban, page 135

MARY HENDERSON
(www.rubylane.com/vintagemerchant
www.etsy.com/shop/TheVintageMerchant)
Western cowgirl blouse, page 51

MICHELLE KOESNADI
(www.glistersandblisters.com
ask@glistersandblisters.com)
Satin gloves, page 131

SIEL DAVOS
(mademoisielleblogspot.com
mademoisielleblog@gmail.com)
Turban, page 4

Glossary

B

bagging out: turning out.

bias: a grain with natural stretch that runs diagonally, at 45 degrees to the selvage.

bishop sleeve: a sleeve that is fitted at the top and gathered into the cuff using flare to make the extra fullness at the cuff.

break line: the line at which the rever naturally folds back.

break point: the point at which the rever starts to fold back to form the lapel.

C

cap sleeve: a very short sleeve. Can be cut in one piece with the body by slightly extending the shoulder line so that it "caps" the shoulder, or can be set in.

collar point: the pointy end of the collar where the lead edge and the leaf edge meet.

construction lines: lines on the pattern giving specific information, such as the dart position.

cut 1 pair: cut one plus a mirrored opposite.

cut 2: cut two identical pieces.

cut to fold/cut on fold: create a mirrored piece from a half-section. Fold a section of fabric and place fold line on pattern to fold. (Do not cut lightweight or jersey fabrics on the fold; instead make a mirrored pattern piece.)

D

darts: a form of suppression found, for example, around the bust, waist, and hips. These are stitched sections, usually triangular or diamond-shaped, that take in areas of excess fabric as shaping.

drape: an amount of extra fabric at the underarm that allows the sleeve to be lifted comfortably. Common in dolman and kimono sleeves.

drill hole: indicates a precise matching or construction point such as the apex of a dart. Marked with chalk or tailor's tacking.

E

ease: an amount of fullness given to a garment to achieve a more comfortable fit. With seams that have been eased in, the excess should be invisible and not gathered.

edgestitch: topstitching sewn close (around ⅛in/3mm) to the edge of the seam or garment profile.

F

fall: the part of the collar that "falls" over, between the roll line and the style line.

flat collar: a collar that sits flat around the shoulders.

fullness: extra fabric added to a pattern piece for shaping that can be used as flare, gather, or ease.

G

grade: to proportionally increase or decrease the size of a pattern.

graded nest: a visual "stack" containing each individual size grade of a pattern piece, from smallest through to largest.

grading: the practice of sizing a pattern piece up or down using set incremental grade rules or measurements.

grain: the thread direction of the fabric. Although it can refer to either warp or weft, the term "grain" is commonly used in connection with the warp.

grainline: a straight line on the pattern piece that denotes the direction in which the pattern should lay, parallel to the warp.

grown on: a pattern piece extended to include another that would normally be cut separately, such as a facing or collar.

grown-on sleeve: a sleeve that is cut in one piece with the body.

I

interfacing: a textile used to stabilize another fabric. These can be either fusible or sewn in, and are available in numerous weights and qualities.

K

kimono sleeve: a sleeve that is cut in one piece with the bodice.

L

lapel: the part of a rever that folds back over the break line and lays flat on the front.

lead edge: the front edge of a collar; for example, the edges on a shirt collar between which the tie would sit.

leaf edge/style line: the outer edge of the collar.

leg-of-mutton: a very full sleeve that is gathered into the armhole and at the elbow. The sleeve is then closely fitted from the elbow to the wrist, forming a leg-of-mutton shape.

lining: the inner shell of a garment, made of a lighter-weight fabric, that encloses all the internal seams.

M

mirrored piece: a symmetrical pattern piece, which, flipped on a mirror line, creates the complete garment section.

miter: to cut away bulk from seam allowances at corners, diagonally, so that they can be turned through fully, ensuring a sharp profile edge.

N

nett: a piece or section of pattern without seam allowance.

nett pattern: a pattern without seam allowance.

notches: small snips made in the seam allowance to mark where two garment pieces are to be matched and sewn together.

P

pile: fabric constructed with a yarn that rises at an angle, such as velvet or corduroy.

profile: the outer edge of a garment or garment section.

Q

quarter-stitch: topstitching ¼in (6mm) in from the profile edge. Seen on shirt collars and cuffs.

R

raglan sleeve: a sleeve that has the shoulder sections of the back and front bodice grown on, making a sleeve that extends up to the neck.

rever: a collar that is partially grown on to the front, and forms a permanent fold-back.

roll: a small amount of extra fabric given to allow a seam to be "rolled" so that the seam edge is hidden. Found, for example, on collars and revers.

S

seam allowance: an extra amount (for example, ½in/1.2cm) added around the pattern to allow for garment pieces to be seamed together.

self/main: the main fabric of the garment.

selvage: the self-finished edges of the fabric (derived from "self-edge").

semi-grown-on sleeve: a sleeve that has part of the body attached to it.

set-in sleeve: a sleeve that is sewn in to a completely made-up arm hole; that is, the shoulder and side seams are sewn before the sleeve is sewn in.

shading: a fabric with a texture such as brocade or satin.

sink-stitch: to stitch "invisibly" into, or through, one seam, to attach another garment part underneath, such as a waistband facing.

sleevehead: the (usually curved) section at the top of a sleeve, which is sewn into the armhole.

sleeve pitch: the correct "hang" of the sleeve. Balance points and accurate cutting will control this.

sloper/block: a basic pattern that can be used as a starting point for drafting many styles of garment.

stand: the part of the collar that stands up around the neck. Usually separate, for example, on shirt collars. It can also be concealed.

suppression: shaping such as darts, tucks, or gathers that take in excess fabric.

T

toile/muslin: a test version of a garment, normally made in calico/muslin.

topstitch: a line of stitch that is seen on the right side of fabric, usually sewn in a larger stitch length with topstitching thread. Topstitching can be both functional (adding strength to seams) and decorative.

turning out: two sections are stitched together, sewing around profile edges with right sides together. With one part left open, the section is then turned through, or "bagged out," enclosing all seams.

twin-needle stitching: two, typically parallel, rows of stitching. Found, for example, on jeans pockets.

W

warp: the lengthwise yarns of a fabric, which run parallel to the edge.

weft: yarns that run across the fabric, at right angles to the edge.

wrap: the extra fabric added onto a collar and center front to enable the fronts to overlap and fasten up.

Further reading

Bibliography

Nigel Cawthorne, *Key Moments in Fashion: The Evolution of Style*, Hamlyn, 2001

Robert Elms, *The Way We Wore: A Life in Threads*, Picador, 2005

James Laver, *Costume and Fashion: A Concise History*, Thames and Hudson, 2002

Joan Nunn, *Fashion in Costume 1200–2000*, New Amsterdam Books, 2000

Vintage Fashion, Carlton Books Limited, 2010

Claire Wilcox, *Twentieth-Century Fashion in Detail*, V&A Publishing, 2009

Harriet Worsley, *Decades of Fashion*, Getty Images, 2006

Useful websites

dressmakingresearch.com
A collection of primary source materials focusing on the cut and construction of women's garments.

queensofvintage.com
Global online magazine for vintage lovers, by vintage lovers.

vintagefashionclub.com
Vintage Fashion Club investigates retro fashion.

vintagefashionguild.org
Dedicated to the promotion and preservation of vintage fashion, with an extensive knowledge base of vintage fashion.

Index

Acknowledgments

Jo would like to extend huge appreciation to RotoVision, and to all those who have contributed to the book, in particular: Lindy Dunlop, Isheeta Mustafi, Nicola Hodgson, Diane Leyman, Sophie O'Kelly, Jo-ann Fortune, and Gemma Seager.

A thank you is extended to Zuhair Alzahr at Grade House. A big shout out is also owed to Miss Loomes, Miss Jenkins, Miss Bloom, and last, but certainly not least, Mr. Freeman.

RotoVision would like to thank Colette Patterns, Siel Davos, Decades of Style Pattern Company, Ann-Marie Faulkner, Carrie Harwood, Mary Henderson, Jacqueline Rose, Audrey Rogers, and Lisa Marshall for contributing their wonderful images.